THE MIRACLES OF CHRIST

Norma Eden

THE MIRACLES OF CHRIST

ARCHBISHOP DMITRI (ROYSTER)

ST VLADIMIR'S SEMINARY PRESS
CRESTWOOD, NEW YORK 10707
1999

Library of Congress Cataloging-in-Publication Data

Royster, Dmitri, 1923-
    The Miracles of Christ / Dmitri Royster.
        p.   cm.
    ISBN 0-88141-193-0 (alk. paper)
    1. Jesus Christ—Miracles.   2. Orthodox Eastern Church—
Liturgy—Calendar.   I. Title.
BT366.R68   1999
226.7'06—dc21

                                                                98-56027
                                                                        CIP

THE MIRACLES OF CHRIST

ISBN 0-88141-193-0

In grateful acknowledgment of the many hours of editorial
work accomplished by Mr. Paul Buckley, Editorial Staff,
Dallas Morning News.

Contents

Part III

FOREWORD

The Miracles of Christ is the third in a series of New Testament studies by Archbishop Dmitri of Dallas (OCA). The first two, also published by SVS Press, are devoted to *The Kingdom of God* and *The Parables*. Excepting the miraculous events in His own life—His birth of the Virgin Mary, His transfiguration on Tabor, His resurrection from the dead, and His ascension—the present study is a commentary on all the "miracles and wonders and signs" of Christ as recorded in the four Gospels.

I

Two basic convictions shape the study. The first has to do with the *miracles* themselves. What place do they occupy in the life and teachings of Jesus Christ? To Archbishop Dmitri this place is clear: any preaching about Christ that omits His miracles or marginalizes their significance makes for a "defective, distorted picture" of His work as Redeemer. The miracles reveal the truth about Jesus' life and person, proving beyond a doubt that He is "what He claimed to be, the Son of God and God incarnate." Referred to as signs (*semeion, dunameis*—terms used throughout the Gospels, especially that of St. John), they point beyond themselves to "the restoration of all things to their pristine state," to the advent of the Kingdom of God, of which Jesus, "attested to of God... by miracles and wonders and signs" (Acts 2:22), is the King.

The study is a careful and at times word-by-word commentary on the Biblical text. It includes analyses of numerous key words from the original Greek, highlighting of differences in the Gospels' parallel accounts of the miracles and relevant citations from many other passages and books of the Bible. This detail, however, does not obscure or diminish the impact of the Biblical narratives. Throughout the commentary they continue to speak for themselves, stirring the reader toward his or her own personal reckoning with Jesus Christ: "The blind receive their sight, and the lame walk, the lepers are cleansed, and the deaf hear, and the dead are raised up, and the poor have the gospel preached to them. And blessed is he, whoever shall not be offended in me" (Matthew 11:5-6 KJV).

No one is excluded from such a reckoning. The miracles of Christ touch upon every kind of person and situation: young people and old; children; men, women and families; people with all kinds of maladies and infirmities—both physical and spiritual; people of faith and those whose faith was far from complete; people who brought themselves to the Lord; people whom no one brought and for whom no one, not even themselves, asked.

The study gives particular attention to the healing of people possessed by demons (the author terms such people as "dehumanized"). These people, socially ostracized, are frequently found dwelling among the dead in cemeteries. Often unclothed, physically powerful and unruly in behavior, they are dangerous to approach. According to Archbishop Dmitri they are "bound by Satan" for reasons additional to the "general law" of *original* sin. Their possession by demons is a result of *their own* sins, of their own abandoning of themselves to these sins and of their own "rejection of dependence on God." These reasons indeed raise thorny issues about the relationships between personal sin, affliction and divine punishment—issues which the Archbishop addresses throughout his study.

He notes too that, significantly, Jesus does not permit the demons which He expels from the possessed to confess His true identity. The Lord's "hour" has not yet come, and in any event, He is in no need of the testimony of demons. In one troubling episode, read in all three of its Synoptic versions during the course of a liturgical year, Jesus does allow the demons He expels to enter into a large herd of swine. To the dismay of the crowd, the swine immediately plunge down a steep hillside and to their death in the sea. Why does Jesus permit such a mass destruction of irrational creatures? Without neglecting to examine the several difficult aspects of this perplexing question, the Archbishop offers a characteristically direct answer: "One thing that the incident makes clear...is the worth in God's eyes of each human being, a worth far greater than that of all the swine in the world."

The miracles touched not only those over whom they were performed but also the bystanders. Many such people, seeing the things that Jesus did, "believed on him" (John 11:45). Other observers were left in confusion or doubt (John 9:21-23), and still others "took counsel to put him to death" (John 11:47-53). Affected too by the miracles were nature and material things such as: the weather, the sea, fish, animals, trees, food and drink, water, and even common earth. Indeed, in the miracles Jesus Christ is shown to be what He is: Lord of everyone and everything.

The study presents especially heedful analysis of the three recorded instances of Jesus raising the dead—Jairus' daughter, the son of the widow of Nain, and the greatest, the raising of Lazarus. In each of these instances the author explains that the "last enemy," death, is being defeated in one of its "successive aspects." Jairus' daughter is raised while still on her deathbed. The son of the widow of Nain is raised while he is being carried to his place of entombment. And Lazarus, the beloved friend over whose tomb Jesus wept and whose body had already begun to corrupt, is raised after being dead four days. These "signs" point to the consummate defeat of death in the death and resurrection of Jesus Christ Himself.

II

The second conviction shaping this study concerns the placement of the miracles of Christ in the liturgy of the Church, that "special society," as Archbishop Dmitri calls it, whose primary task down through the ages has been to remember and proclaim, without defect or distortion, the truth about Jesus— His life, person, teachings and works. When are the miracle narratives read and celebrated in the course of a liturgical year? The Archbishop's response regarding this matter is unequivocal: the liturgical placement of the miracle accounts does not reflect "random choice," but rather a "carefully planned pattern of lessons" connecting their content to appropriate days, cycles and seasons within the liturgical year. About this "pattern of lessons," or lectionary as it is commonly known, a few words of general introduction are in order.[1]

For its use in Orthodox worship, the Gospel is fashioned as a liturgical book. In the course of a liturgical year (from Pascha to Pascha) all four Gospels are read in the following sequence: John, Matthew, Luke and Mark (with considerable overlapping along the way). The separate readings (lesson numbers) are selected and arranged so that each best suits the distinct type of liturgical day for which it is prescribed: Saturdays,

1 The Gospel lectionary is a matter of significant discussion among clergy and laity in both the Orthodox Church and the Eastern-Rite Catholic Churches. For insights into this debate, two recent articles in the *St. Vladimir's Theological Quarterly* may be consulted: Paul Meyendorff, "The Liturgical Path of Orthodoxy in America," 40, 1-2 (1996) and David M. Petras, "The Gospel Lectionary of the Byzantine Church," 41, 2-3 (1997). About the details of the lectionary, and differences between Slavic and Greek usages, an old but still helpful study may be found in: *Eastern Churches Quarterly*, Irmgard M. deVries, "The Epistles, Gospels and Tones of the Byzantine Liturgical Year," X, 1, 2, 3, 4 (1953).

Sundays, weekdays, and feastdays or days within special festal cycles. The weekday readings are most reflective of a *lectio continua*. The narratives of the Lord's postresurrectional appearances are collected into a separate cycle of eleven lessons which is read through at Sunday Matins four to five times per year.

Archbishop Dmitri notes that, within the above-described "pattern of lessons," most of the miracles of Christ are proclaimed and celebrated on Sundays, especially on those 32 which fall during the longest segment of the liturgical year—a season known as the time "after Pentecost." It should be noted that this segment may extend to as many as 37 weeks when the earliest day of Pascha is followed directly by the latest date for this great feast. Within the basic number of 32, however, fully *17* of the Sunday readings are devoted to the miracles.

The author sees nothing unusual or surprising in this development. He explains that this segment of the annual cycle is the time of the Church's mission to the world—a mission renewed each year at Pentecost and continuing until the Lord's Second Coming. The sequence of miracle narratives appointed for its principal days, Sundays, "reflects the content of the Apostles' proclamation, which must be the content of the Church's proclamation in every age, not least our own."

The liturgical year's shortest section, termed "of Pascha" in the liturgical calendars, is always composed of eight weeks. Its shape and content emerge from the first several centuries of the Church's life and worship, when Pascha was the primary day for baptism. The eight weeks which followed were devoted to the mystagogical instruction of the newly-baptized in the sacramental-liturgical mysteries into which they, after lengthy preparation, had been initiated. The Gospel readings for this season became fixed as those from John, since his Gospel is replete with acts of faith and belief in Jesus as Lord, and

with references to those material things and human circumstances—water, bread, wine, washing, forgiveness of sins,
walking, hearing, gaining sight, marriage and other *semeia*—
most commonly encountered and sanctified in the sacramental
ministrations and liturgical celebrations of the Church. Such
features are especially evident in the Sunday readings of this
period "of Pascha."

The third section of the liturgical year is a fixed period of
ten weeks of preparation prior to Pascha. In this season a special liturgical book known as the Lenten Triodion is employed
and, in most instances, the Gospel of Mark is read. Gospel lessons during the Great Fast are limited almost exclusively to
Saturdays and Sundays, since lenten weekdays generally have
no prescribed Gospel readings. Drawing the liturgical year to a
close, then, these readings fulfill two primary purposes. They
address some of the many conflicts between Jesus and the
Pharisees and Scribes over fidelity to the law of Moses (especially the Saturday readings). And in the lessons about Christ's
miracles they offer an adequate summary of the basics of the
faith and the newness of life given once and for all in baptism.

III

The two convictions outlined above, along with ample citations
from liturgical hymns, sacramental prayers and more than a
dozen Church Fathers, especially St. John Chrysostom, St.
Ambrose of Milan and the Blessed Theophylact, together offer
considerable insight into the manner in which the miracles of
Christ are received and understood by Orthodox Christians.
The miracles serve as compelling testimony to Jesus of Nazareth,
the Son of God and Redeemer, who performed them. Within
the Church's "liturgical experience," His work continues to be
remembered, proclaimed and extended. "Liturgical experience"
is an overused and often ambiguous term, but Archbishop

Dmitri gives it clarity and scope by linking it, as the Church Fathers did, "to baptism and the eucharist, since it is quite clear from the Acts of the Apostles and the epistles that these mysteries were the preeminent elements in the life of the early Church."[2] And to this day they remain preeminent in the Orthodox Church as the sacraments of reckoning with Christ, i.e., of repentance, conversion and communion.

A final word in this foreword has to do with "great love and compassion"cited numerous times by Archbishop Dmitri as the ultimate motive behind not only every one of Jesus' miracles but also behind the whole of God's miraculous plan for the salvation of all human beings and the entire world. As the evangelist Matthew writes: "And when he saw the multitudes, he was moved with compassion on them, because they fainted, and were scattered abroad, as sheep having no shepherd" (Matthew 9:36).

An analogous love and compassion are also evident throughout this excellent study of the miracles of Christ. They emanate from the heart of its author, who is himself a wise, scholarly and devoted archpastor and teacher of the Church.

Fr. Paul Lazor
December 4, 1998

2 For the views of St. Irenaeus, St. Athanasius, St. Basil and others on these matters, see Georges Florovsky, "The Function of Tradition in the Ancient Church," in *Bible, Church, Tradition: An Eastern Orthodox View*, (Nordland Publishing Co., Belmont, MA, 1972).

INTRODUCTION

Our Lord Jesus Christ began His public ministry with a call to repentance, and immediately He told His hearers why they must give heed. They must reorient their whole life, He said, "for the kingdom of heaven is at hand." John the Baptist had issued the same call and the same admonition. Jesus' repetition of it at the very beginning unquestionably authenticates John's work and confirms his relation to Jesus as His forerunner. The Lord's prophet, the last and greatest, prophesies. Jesus Christ fulfills.

No greater reason for the need of repentance is possible, if by "the kingdom of heaven is at hand" we understand that God Himself has come to reclaim His creation and exercise His lordship over the human race. In other words, heaven—that is, God—will reign, and He will become King indeed. This coming had been promised by Israel's history and Israel's prophets. Jesus Christ is the promised and expected Redeemer and Savior.

Because Jesus Christ was God incarnate, His very presence made the assertion "is at hand" (or "has drawn near") a literal fact: where God is, there is the kingdom. Still, He will reign in the hearts of men and women who repent; He will not force His reign upon those who reject Him.

The theme announced by Jesus at the outset of His ministry remained the theme throughout. The Sermon on the Mount, the Lord's first extended discourse, describes the kind of reorientation that is necessary for entering into the kingdom of heaven both in this life and in the life of the age to come. All the parables that the Lord used to illustrate His truth can be

1

called parables of the kingdom, even if only some of them begin with such expressions as "the kingdom of heaven is like..." The point is that the parables show by means of situations drawn from the people's experience how things will be when God's reign is complete. It is also to be noted that in the forty days between the resurrection and the ascension, not only did the Lord's disciples experience the kingdom by His very presence but He also spoke to them about "things pertaining to the kingdom of God" (Acts 1:3). By this time, they surely understood that the Lord meant three things by "the kingdom of God": His reign in the hearts of men; His special society, the Church, made up of those who obey His reign; and the fullness of His reign in the world or age to come.

The proclamation of the kingdom in word (direct teaching or parable) is supported by proclamation in deed—signs that manifest God's final victory over the evil one and his confederates, who strive to prevent God's reign in human hearts. These signs are Christ's miracles. The Gospels report some of them in considerable detail: persons, times, places, and other circumstances. Others are referred to more generally: "He healed their sick." "Jesus went about... healing all manner of sickness and all manner of disease among the people," etc.

Twentieth-century skeptics reject the authenticity of the Lord's miracles outright. Even some biblical scholars have declared them impossible. Others have been tempted to write them off as the mythological "clothing" common to religious expression at the time the Gospels were written. Still others have imagined that the "original" forms of the Gospel narrations lacked a miraculous element and that they were embellished as faith in the divinity of Christ developed. Our impression is that most of these interpreters approach the Gospels as outsiders and do not see them from within as part of the living Tradition of the Church. They separate the New Testament from the Church, on which even they must depend for its transmission, content, and authenticity.

The skeptics miss yet another point. The Gospels tell us, in passages not easily discarded as late additions, that many of the people who believed in Christ did so because of His miracles. These believers include His own disciples, some Gentiles, and even those otherwise inclined to be His enemies, the Jews.

A few examples: "This beginning of signs (miracles) did Jesus in Cana of Galilee, and manifested forth His glory; and His disciples believed on Him" (John 2:11). A "certain nobleman" who begged Jesus to come down and heal his son knew that the fever had left him "at the same hour, in the which Jesus said unto him, Thy son liveth: and himself believed, and his whole house" (John 4:53). "Now when He was in Jerusalem at the Passover, in the feast day, many believed in His name, when they saw the miracles which He did" (John 2:23). "Then many of the Jews which came to Mary (Lazarus' sister), and had seen the things which Jesus did, believed on Him" (John 11:45).

The New Testament has built in its own attestation to or authentication of the miracles. On the other hand, there is no evidence that the Lord sought to make Himself known as a miracle-worker, or that He simply dazzled the crowds. The best word to describe our Lord's works in which He departed from the natural order is *sign* (Greek, *semeion*). The fourth Gospel uses this word exclusively, and even the word used by the other Gospel authors, *dunameis* ("power"), points to a breakthrough of God's power and His dominion and reign over all things.

The miracles, then, are signs that point to something—a truth—far greater and more important than the acts themselves: the restoration of all things to their pristine state, the way things were supposed to be or should have developed if men had obeyed God's will in the first place.

During a large part of the church year, between All Saints Sunday and the Sunday of the Publican and the Pharisee, each Sunday is numbered from the first to the thirty-second after Pentecost, with corresponding epistle and Gospel lessons to be read at the Divine Liturgy. (If Pascha comes very early, there may be more than thirty-two "Sundays after Pentecost"; the lessons for those additional Sundays generally repeat the lessons already read on their proper Sundays.) The fact that these Sundays are numbered from Pentecost is significant: on Pentecost, the fiftieth day after Pascha, the Church celebrates the memorial of the Descent of the Holy Spirit. (When the Church celebrates a memorial, she not only remembers but also relives in liturgical actions the event commemorated.) This was the day when the Church was born and sent forth in accordance with the Savior's promise: "Ye shall receive power, after that the Holy Spirit is come upon you, and ye shall be witnesses unto me both in Jerusalem, and in all Judea, and in Samaria, and unto the uttermost part of the earth" (Acts 1:8). For the Apostles, the time after Pentecost was the time of the Church in the world, the time when they carried out their mission. The book of the Acts of the Apostles is the record of the Church in the first days of its existence doing the work she was empowered and sent to do. It is the record of the Apostles' and their disciples' witness to Christ.

The power and the commission were not given to the Apostles only. These belong to the Church in every age. In our Lord's prayer before His glorification, that is, His crucifixion and resurrection, He prayed for the Apostles (John 17:6). But He very pointedly said that what He asked of the Father was not for them exclusively: "Neither pray I for these alone, but for them also which shall believe on me through their word" (v. 20).

When the Church relives the experience of Pentecost every year, her people renew their commitment to preaching Christ as well as to living in accordance with His commandments and to teaching all nations to do the same (Matthew 28:19, 20).

The content of that preaching and teaching is this: that Christ has come into the world, and that in His coming the kingdom of God is at hand. Christ, the Son of God, literally brought God's reign to mankind, and His presence continues in the Church, His mystical body, for He said: "As the Father hath sent me, even so send I you" (John 20:21). The men and women who constitute the Church on earth live and move in anticipation of the fullness of the kingdom in the world to come. It is in the eucharist, the Divine Liturgy, that they participate here and now in that kingdom to come.

The Sundays after Pentecost, then, are the period of the Church's mission to the world. The Gospel lessons appointed to be read during this time reflect the content of the Apostles' proclamation, which must be the content of the Church's proclamation in every age, not least our own. These lessons are taken from the Holy Gospels of St. Matthew and St. Luke. There is nothing arbitrary about the selection. Unfortunately, one hears from time to time a complaint that the lessons are not varied enough and the suggestion that a revision of the lectionary is in order. Even more unfortunately, one hears another complaint: that "too many" lessons deal with the miracles of our Lord.

Perhaps such dissatisfaction betrays, especially in our times, a distaste for the miraculous in the accounts our Lord's public ministry. Ours is a highly secularized society, and a Christ without miracles might be more palatable. But the Church stands firm in her conviction that the work of Christ, which included His miracles, proved Him to be what He claimed to be: "I and the Father are one" (John 10:30).

We insist that the Gospel readings for the Divine Liturgy do not reflect a random choice. Rather, we are dealing with a definite, carefully planned pattern of lessons appropriate to the lengthy season after Pentecost. Before discussing the miracles they recount (as well as the miracles they do not), we should like to list the lessons in question and say a word or two about their content.

I

1

READINGS FOR THE SUNDAYS AFTER PENTECOST

First Sunday (Matthew 10:22-32, 37-38; 19:27-30): Our Lord Jesus Christ tells His disciples simply and directly what is required of any who would follow Him: they must confess Him before men and not deny Him; they can love no one more than Him; they must take up their cross and follow Him; and they must leave all for His sake.

Second Sunday (Matthew 4:18-23): Going back in time, we have a record of the call of the first Apostles. We see how, at Jesus' bidding, they left everything immediately to follow Him. They could not have known then all that would be required of them. That would become clearer in the course of their daily life with Him.

Third Sunday (Matthew 6:22-33): Again our Lord explains the nature of discipleship: the follower of Christ cannot have divided purposes or loyalties; he cannot be over-anxious, even about life's necessities; he must seek first the kingdom of God and have faith that God will provide.

These first three lessons make it clear that in proclaiming Christ to the world, the disciples had to be faithful to these strict, essential requirements and, in turn, convey them to all. They could not make half-hearted converts. The Church's mission in our own time is the same. She cannot preach an adjusted or diluted message to gain followers. She cannot compromise with those who want to compromise with the world.

The next seven lessons are miracle accounts. Their purpose is two-fold. They prove that Christ is the Son of God, powerful over all things. He heals sicknesses, restores sight, casts out demons, and exercises lordship over creation. They likewise show that those who enter His kingdom (becoming members of His Body, the Church, and letting Christ reign in their hearts) lead a miraculous life, once their spiritual ills are cured. The preaching of Christ, if it is to be authentic, cannot ignore His "miracles and wonders and signs," as St. Peter teaches us in his first sermon (Acts 2:22).

Fourth Sunday (Matthew 8:5-13): Jesus heals the servant of a centurion (a Gentile), whose faith and compassion amaze the Lord.

Fifth Sunday (Matthew 8:28-34; 9:1): Jesus heals two persons possessed with devils and dispatches the devils into a herd of swine. The incident provokes the townspeople to ask Him to leave.

Sixth Sunday (Matthew 9:1-8): Jesus heals a man sick of the palsy, first granting him forgiveness. This He does to prove His power to forgive sins.

Seventh Sunday (Matthew 9:27-35): Sight is restored to two blind men, who recognize Jesus as "the son of David." The Lord then casts out a devil and is accused of casting out devils "through the prince of the devils."

Eighth Sunday (Matthew 14:14-22): Jesus heals the sick people among a multitude following Him. He then miraculously feeds more than five thousand people with five loaves and two fish.

Ninth Sunday (Matthew 14:22-34): The Lord walks on the sea and invites Peter to come to Him. Peter's faith fails as he walks on the water. The Lord calms the storm.

Tenth Sunday (Matthew 17:14-23): The disciples are unable to cure the epileptic son of a certain man. Jesus heals him and rebukes the disciples for their lack of faith.

The next six lessons recount four parables and two incidents. The parables are "of the kingdom," two of them beginning with the words, "the kingdom of heaven is likened to..." The two real incidents are a kind of break in the continuity of "kingdom lessons," but both are occasions for resuming the exposition of essential characteristics of the life in Christ: the Lord's teachings concerning the observance of the commandments.

Eleventh Sunday (Matthew 18:23-35): The Parable of the Unforgiving Servant.

Twelfth Sunday (Matthew 19:16-26): A young man asks what he must do to have eternal life. The Lord tells him he must keep the commandments. The man says he has kept the commandments and asks what he still lacks, and Jesus tells him to sell all that he has and give to the poor.

Thirteenth Sunday (Matthew 21:33-42): The Parable of the Vineyard.

Fourteenth Sunday (Matthew 22:2-14): The Parable of the Marriage Feast of the King's Son.

Fifteenth Sunday (Matthew 22:35-46): The Lord, answering a lawyer, declares which are the greatest commandments of the law: love of God and love of neighbor. Jesus identifies Himself as the one whom David called Lord.

Sixteenth Sunday (Matthew 25:14-30): The Parable of the Talents.

As we observed above, the first three Gospel lessons show what it means to be a disciple. The next seven reveal the impact of Christ's presence, or what life is like in the kingdom. A series of four parables teaches us about forgiveness (Eleventh Sunday) and about the use of God's gifts (Sixteenth Sunday), essential teachings for the Christian life. The other two parables deal with the wickedness or sloth that causes loss of membership in the kingdom.

Seventeenth Sunday (Matthew 15:21-28): The healing of the daughter of a woman of Canaan. The Lord does not at first heed her cry for mercy, but when He sees her great faith, expressed in extremely humble terms, He heals her daughter.

Eighteenth Sunday (Luke 5:1-11): The account of the miracle of the great catch of fish. The disciples are taught that they must trust and obey when the Lord commands. He promises to make them fishers of men.

Nineteenth Sunday (Luke 6:31-36): The Lord instructs His disciples, expressing the essence of the Christian life: "as ye would that men should do to you, do ye also to them likewise." The Christian is to love his enemies, do good to those who do him wrong, and even lend without expecting to be repaid.

Twentieth Sunday (Luke 7:11-16): The story of the miracle of raising a widowed mother's only son from the dead. This miracle He does without being asked, but out of His compassion for her.

Twenty-first Sunday (Luke 8:5-15): The Parable of the Sower of Seeds. At the request of His disciples, the Lord, contrary to His custom, explains this parable. It describes the way in which the sowing of the word of God will be received by different people.

Twenty-second Sunday (Luke 16:19-31): The Parable of the Rich Man and Lazarus: The rich man goes to hell after his death because of his misuse of riches, and Lazarus goes to heaven for his patient endurance of his abject poverty. It is to be noted that the sequence of Lucan lessons is broken. We jump from Chapter 8 to Chapter 16, but on the following Sunday the sequence is taken up again.

Twenty-third Sunday (Luke 8:27-39): A man possessed of devils is healed. This is St. Luke's version of the miracle recorded in Matthew 8 (see *Fifth Sunday*). Only one man, rather than two, is mentioned, but the Lord's allowing the devils to enter a herd of swine indicates that it is the same incident. The reaction of the townspeople is significant.

Twenty-fourth Sunday (Luke 8:41-56): Two miracles are recorded here. At the earnest appeal of Jairus for the Lord to heal his daughter, the Lord consents to go to her. This is the second account of His raising someone from the dead. On the way, a woman suffering from an issue of blood for twelve years is healed when she touches the border of His garment.

Twenty-fifth Sunday (Luke 10:25-37): A lawyer asks the Lord what he must do to inherit eternal life and is told to love God and neighbor. "And who is my neighbor?" he asks. The Lord answers with the Parable of the Good Samaritan.

Twenty-sixth Sunday (Luke 12:16-21): Another parable: a rich man whose ground produced so abundantly thought only of storing up his goods to insure a carefree future. He died the very night after he made his plans.

Twenty-seventh Sunday (Luke 13:10-17): The Lord heals a woman who suffered eighteen years with "a spirit of infirmity." His adversaries condemn Him for working on the Sabbath, and He replies with an important lesson.

Twenty-eighth Sunday (Luke 14:16-24): The Parable of the Great Supper, an allegory concerning the response of the chosen people to the Lord's coming.

Twenty-ninth Sunday (Luke 17:12-19): Jesus responds to a cry for help from ten lepers and heals them. Only one, a Samaritan, returns to thank God for what had happened.

Thirtieth Sunday (Luke 18:18-27): A fifth lesson in which the Lord is asked, "What shall I do to inherit eternal life?" (See Sundays 12, 15, 19, and 25). Here the questioner is a rich ruler, who keeps the commandments but asks further, "What do I lack yet?" When the Lord tells him that, in his case, he must sell his goods and give to the poor and follow Him, He goes away sorrowful because He cannot part with his riches. The fact that this question or one very similar to it is the subject of five of the thirty-two lessons is very significant.

Thirty-first Sunday (Luke 18:35-43): The final miracle narrative of the seventeen in the thirty-two Sundays. Jesus restores sight to a blind man who recognizes Him as the Son of David.

Thirty-second Sunday (Luke 19:1-10): Zacchaeus, the rich chief of the publicans (tax collectors), who were considered evil and dishonest social outcasts, overcomes all obstacles to see Jesus. His promise to give half of his goods to the poor and to restore what he has taken falsely moves the Lord to declare, "Today salvation is come into this house." This lesson is read on the Sunday before the Lenten Triodion (the service book for the Great Fast) is taken up.

As we see in our survey of the second half of the Sunday Gospels for the Pentecost season, ten lessons treat miracles. Four contain parables, one is a portion of the Lord's direct instruction to His disciples on doing unto others as they would have them do to them, and the other relates the incident in which a rich ruler asks what he must do to inherit eternal life.

2

THE FOURTH SUNDAY

The Centurion's Servant (Matthew 8:5-13)

The first of the seventeen miracles recounted in the Gospel readings for "the Sundays after Pentecost" is from the eighth chapter of St. Matthew's Gospel. It is the story of a centurion, a Gentile, who intercedes on behalf of his ailing servant. (Note that we are not attempting to present our Lord's miracles chronologically. Rather, we are dealing with those that occur in the lectionary for this period.)

The Lord's signs and wonders prove Him to be what He claimed to be, the Son of God. But the present miracle account, like all others, is not intended solely to demonstrate the Lord's power to heal. The healing of the centurion's servant contains a number of short lessons concerning characteristics of the life in Christ. Christians who hear or read this short section of the Gospel must be attentive to the way in which these instructions may be applied to their own lives.

The basic elements of the story are few. The centurion, a Roman, has complete confidence that Jesus is able to heal his servant. When the Lord expresses willingness to go to his house, the centurion humbly objects, declaring himself unworthy of such a visit. At the same time, he reveals his profound faith in Jesus: "Speak the word only, and my servant shall be healed." He then explains his status as a centurion—he has soldiers under him and is himself under authority. The Lord's reaction must have surprised those who witnessed the scene. He declares that He has not found such great faith in Israel; those chosen to be the children of the kingdom would be cast out and replaced by others. Finally, He tells the centurion to go his way and that his servant is healed. St. Ambrose sees the healing by the Lord's word alone as proof of His equality with the Father: "...as the Father spoke the Son made, so, too, the Father works and the Son speaks" (*On the Holy Spirit*, Book 2, no. 3). And St. Basil the Great emphasizes that it was the Savior's word and not His presence that healed the sick man (*Letter 41*, no. 2).

The centurion is a striking figure. He enters the narrative as a man already possessed of a deep faith in Jesus' power to heal, even by a word. He asks nothing for himself but only for his servant, his social and military inferior. His status notwithstanding, he feels profoundly his own unworthiness.

How the centurion came to his faith is not explained by St. Matthew, but details in St. Luke's account of the same miracle may offer a clue. It should be recalled at this point that although the synoptic Gospels—Matthew, Mark, and Luke—sometimes differ in detail when reporting the same incident, those differences do not diminish their authenticity. In the present case, St. Matthew simply relates what went on between Jesus and the centurion; St. Luke tells us of certain preliminary steps, such as the centurion's dispatching his Jewish friends to plead his case. "Neither thought I myself worthy to come unto thee," he says (Luke 7:7). The centurion's frequent contacts with the Jews must have given him some familiarity with their faith; perhaps he was aware of their messianic expectations. It is unlikely that Jesus and His work among the people could have escaped his attention. His own faith, so forcefully portrayed in just a few words, may have arisen from a strong sense that Jesus was the very one awaited by the nation he had come to love.

St. Luke's account tells us that the man's Jewish friends—identified as elders—considered him worthy of Jesus' good favor, although they are impressed by something other than his faith. "He was worthy for whom He should do this: for he loveth our nation, and he hath built us a synagogue" (7:4-5). They present a plea from a man who has an exalted position and has contributed materially to their institution. The things that really matter—the centurion's humility, faith, and concern for another—seem not to have made much of an impression on them. It is not difficult to see the similarity between the mind of those religious leaders and that of some in our own times. And not a few pastors have heard requests on behalf of others who were deemed worthy for the wrong reasons.

Clearly, when the centurion speaks to Jesus of his position, he is not boasting. Quite the contrary. "I am a man under authority." That is the key expression. He derives his authority from another and applies it in the line of duty. St. John Chrysostom describes the implications: " 'I also am a man set under authority': that is, Thou art God, and I man; I under authority, but Thou not under authority. If I, therefore, being a man, and under authority, can do so much (complete command over his soldiers); far more He, both as God and as not under authority" (*On the Gospel According to St. Matthew*, Homily 26). The same saint is certain that this Gentile, unlike his Jewish friends, suspects Jesus' divine dignity.

The Christ preached by the Apostles was the Christ who gave Himself out of love for mankind. He is the One who receives all who come to Him in faith and humility, those who love Him. He is not moved to respond to our petitions because of some supposed worthiness on our part. Our accomplishments, position, wealth, and fame do not commend us to Him. Neither does our belonging to a particular race or nation, and neither does membership in His Church when we make no effort to live in accordance with His will, have no faith or humility, think of ourselves as deserving His salvation, or think only of ourselves and never earnestly desire the well-being of others. Such was the image of Christ that the apostles and disciples proclaimed as they undertook their great missionary enterprise after having been filled with the Holy Spirit at Pentecost. For St. Gregory of Nazianzus, the centurion's faith and approach to the Lord provide an example for us all: "Wherefore we must purify ourselves first, and then approach this converse with the Pure...be like the Centurion who would seek for healing, but would not, through a praiseworthy fear, receive the Healer into his house. Let each one of us also speak so, as long as he is still uncleansed, and is a Centurion still, commanding many in wickedness, and serving in the army of Caesar, the World-ruler of those who are being dragged down; 'I am not worthy that thou shouldest enter under my roof'" (*Oration on the Holy Lights*, 9).

3

THE FIFTH SUNDAY

The Healing of the Demoniacs (Matthew 8:28-34; 9:1)
On the Fifth Sunday after Pentecost, the reading from the Holy Gospel is the 28th Section of St. Matthew (8:28-34; 9:1). In it

our Lord heals two persons possessed by devils. The same miracle is found in Mark 5:1-17 and in Luke 8:27-39, the latter being the reading for the Twenty-third Sunday.

At its very beginning, Jesus' work is described as consisting of two parts: "preaching the gospel of the kingdom, and healing all manner of sickness and disease among the people" (Matthew 4:23). He cured not only those who suffered from physical illnesses but also those who were possessed (v. 24). Among the latter cases, one of the earliest is the healing of the two "in the country of the Gergesenes" (or Gadarenes, according to St. Mark and St. Luke). St. Mark and St. Luke mention one man, rather than two. Few Orthodox commentators see any inconsistency in this. The Blessed Theophylact gives the explanation most often found in the writings of the Church Fathers: "Understand that this one man was one of the two mentioned by Matthew, evidently the more notorious of the two" (*The Explanation of the Holy Gospel According to St. Matthew*, ch. 8, v. 28).

The Church's preaching of Christ to the world cannot omit mention of His power over demons and His casting them out. It is an essential part of His work. He, the eternal Word of God, became man to destroy the devil's hold on mankind. "For this purpose the Son of God was manifested, that He might destroy the works of the devil" (1 John 3:8).

Demon possession, unlike some physical sickness, is understood as the consequence of one's own sins, of his abandoning himself to sin, ending up in moral depravity, and of his rejection of dependence on God. However gradual the process may be, the taking over by evil spirits eventually is complete and destructive. In our own time, the possibility of demon possession is acknowledged by many, although only a few decades ago most educated people ridiculed the idea.

The picture of the possessed drawn by the three Evangelists

deserves careful attention, for it is symptomatic of all cases in any period of history: the possessed is dehumanized.

St. Matthew (8:28) writes of two men and notes two phenomena: their "coming out of the tombs" and their being "exceeding fierce."

St. Mark (5:1-5) records other details. The possessed had "his dwelling among the tombs; and no man could bind him, no, not with chains." The latter condition is further explained: "Because he had often been bound with fetters and chains, and the chains had been plucked asunder by him, and the fetters broken in pieces: neither could any man tame him." His less-than-human condition is described thus: "And always, night and day, he was in the mountains, and in the tombs, crying, and cutting himself with stones."

From St. Luke (8:25, 29) we learn that he "ware no clothes, neither abode in any house, but in the tombs...for oftentimes it (the unclean spirit) had caught him: and he was kept bound with chains and in fetters; and he brake the bands, and was driven of the devil into the wilderness."

All three Gospels report that the possessed dwelt in or among the tombs. The implications are enormous. Living in the tombs or among the dead would have been repugnant to the Jews. Dead men's bones were unclean; touching them rendered one unclean and made a purification necessary. But there is more to it than that.

Perhaps of even greater importance is the condition of the possessed—a preoccupation with the dead and spirits of the dead. Nothing is more characteristic in our times of "new age" adherents and the sects than this preoccupation. Spirits under the domination of the devil communicate with the living and act as guides to them in their quest to become gods. In the Gospel account, the possessed were no longer fit to live in normal society, thus the preference for cemeteries and the mountains or wilderness.

Another remarkable characteristic of the possessed is their super-human strength, which made them a threat to anyone who came close. In our modern experience, this super-human strength is manifested mentally and spiritually. Agents of the devil often possess great power, have persuasive influence over others, and, aided by the devil himself, even perform miracles. Some even claim to do God's work. The formula for discerning whether these spirits be of God is given by the Apostle John in his first epistle: "Every spirit that confesseth not that Jesus Christ is come in the flesh is not of God: and this is that antichrist (or spirit of antichrist), whereof ye have heard that it should come; and even now already is it in the world" (4:3).

That the possessed wore no clothes is further evidence of separation from the company of others. Another testimony to his dehumanized condition is his crying (shrieking), undoubtedly with unintelligible sounds. From the fact that he cut himself with stones, we see that he had become his own worst enemy, that he was bent on self-destruction, the ultimate consequence of the devil's possession.

Regarding the specific Gospel lesson being considered (Matthew 8:28-34), it is interesting to note that no one brought the two possessed men to the Lord. Indeed, no one dared go near them. It seems that Jesus went out to meet them Himself, and when they saw Him they came.

The immediate response to His presence is amazing. "What have we (or "have I" in Mark and Luke) to do with thee, Jesus, thou Son of God? Art thou come hither to torment us before the time?" The most remarkable thing is that the devils know that Jesus is the Son of God and recognize Him as the enemy. "What have we to do with thee?" Their purpose was man's destruction; His was mankind's salvation.

Their question—"Art thou come hither to torment us before the time?"—leaves no doubt that they know their destiny.

What they do not want to face is their destruction "before the time," the time appointed for their destruction (see Revelation 14:10 and 20:10). They have succeeded in reducing these men to a subhuman level, but they have not completed their work. When the Lord commands them to come out, they even ask not to be destroyed, at least not yet. As St. Luke expresses it, "They besought Him that He would not command them to go out into the deep."

The next part of the story, in which they ask to be allowed to enter the large herd of swine that were feeding on the mountain, has caused commentators no little difficulty. Why do the demons propose something so extraordinary, since, in fact, humanity was the object of their destructive work? More difficult to answer is why the Lord permits it. The Fathers generally agree that, in spite of the devastating results of the devils' possession of these men, it was God's providential care that prevented their self-destruction. Contrary to what the devils expect, they have no power over the swine. The swine, irrational creatures, cannot become servants of the devil and thus cannot even tolerate his presence. Most unexpectedly, the swine's mass suicide becomes the instrument of the very destruction the devils feared.

The Lord's allowing this thing to happen has been judged "inhumane" by some modern commentators. One thing that the incident makes clear—and this perhaps is not acceptable to certain activists in our time—is the worth in God's eyes of each human being, a worth far greater than that of all the swine in the world. It is also evident that man, a rational being with a free will, can be reduced by demon possession to a dehumanized condition. The pigs, on the other hand, could not be reduced to any lower condition, even by being taken over by demons. Further, swine were unclean and worthless as far as the Jews were concerned. And one may wonder why there was a herd of swine in the first place. Perhaps the country was Gentile territory. It has been suggested that the Jews, to their shame, were keeping these unclean beasts for profit.

In any case, this remains an unusual turn of events, as even the Fathers noted. St. John Chrysostom suggests that our Lord wished to provide visible proof that He really had cast the demons out (*On the Gospel According to St. Matthew*, Homily 28, no. 4). Otherwise, since Christ had been accused of casting out devils in the devil's name, He might have been suspected of some magical trick or of casting a spell over the men in question. Most important, it was the Lord's purpose to show that the devils had not power even over swine. Speaking of the devil's temptation of Job, St. Athanasius says: "...although willing he could not prevail against one just man. For if he could have, he would not have asked permission. And it is no wonder if he could do nothing against Job, when destruction would not have come even on his cattle, had not God allowed it. And he has not the power over swine, for as it is written in the Gospel, they besought the Lord, saying, 'Let us enter the swine.' But if they had power not even against swine, much less have they any over men formed in the image of God" (*Life of St. Antony*, no. 24). This truth is brought home to all who enter the holy Church, for they have this rebuke addressed to the devil: "Acknowledge the vainness of thy might, which hath not power even over swine" (Prayers at the Reception of Catechumens, Second Exorcism).

Both St. Mark and St. Luke present a picture of the man after the cure: "They (the people of the city) went out to see what was done; and came to Jesus, and found the man, out of whom the devils were departed, sitting at the feet of Jesus, clothed, and in his right mind: and they were afraid" (Luke 8:35). The devil's grip is broken, and the man has regained his integral human condition. He even makes an effort to remain with the Lord, follow Him, and perhaps become one of His disciples.

The Lord wills otherwise, however: "Return to thine own house, and show how great things God hath done unto thee." His calling is now to be, if you will, a lay witness to God's saving and transforming power.

The townspeople might have been happy, or at least indifferent, about the man's restoration, had it not cost them. How important the swine were to their economy we cannot really know. But the loss, coupled with the fear they felt in the face of God's power, prompts them to ask the Lord "to depart out of their coasts."

St. John Chrysostom calls them "a sort of senseless people" (ibid.). "They could not bear the presence of Christ," says St. Ambrose, because of their materialism ("Sermon Against Auxentius," no. 20). In that respect, they were probably not much different from the people in most of our cities today. How many would gladly suffer economic loss, individual or general, if it meant that one person or a whole class could be healed, restored, or relieved of some wretched condition? How many would tolerate the disturbance of their "way of life" by the concrete evidence of the mighty work of God in their midst?

4

THE SIXTH SUNDAY

The Paralytic (Matthew 9:1-8)

The Gospel lesson for the Sixth Sunday after Pentecost is the 29th Section of St. Matthew's Gospel. It records the healing of a man "sick of the palsy," or a paralytic. St. Mark also records the miracle, and his account (2:1-12) is read on the Second Sunday of the Great Fast (Lent). All three synoptic Gospels, in fact, record the incident, St. Luke's account being found in 5:18-26.

Although there are differences in detail, as one might expect when three people, even those whose work is guided by the Holy Spirit, report the same incident, the Evangelists are all agreed with regard to what is most significant. They agree that our Lord cured the paralytic because "certain of the scribes said within themselves, This man blasphemeth. Jesus, knowing their thoughts, said, Wherefore think ye evil in your hearts? For whether is easier to say, thy sins be forgiven thee; or to say, Arise and walk? But that ye may know that the Son of man hath power on earth to forgive sins, (then saith He to the sick of the palsy) Arise..."

All three Evangelists indicate, too, that the Lord was moved to respond by the faith of the four men who carried the paralytic into His presence. Perhaps it may be inferred that the sick man likewise had faith in Jesus' power to cure since, although he was helpless, he perhaps consented to being taken to Him. In any case, an important lesson for us is that God honors the intercessory work of faith on behalf of others. "What then does the Lord do? Having seen their faith—not that of the paralytic, but of the bearers; for it is possible for one to be healed by the faith of others; or, perceiving that the paralytic also believed, He healed him" (St. Cyril of Alexandria, *Commentary on the Gospel of St. Luke*, homily on verses from ch. 5). "The bearers believed, and the sick of the palsy enjoyed the blessing of the cure" (St. Cyril of Jerusalem, *Catechetical Lecture 5*, no. 8).

Although St. Matthew does not mention the extraordinary means to which the paralytic's friends resorted, both St. Mark and St. Luke do: the friends could not come into Jesus' presence because of the crowd, so they went up to the roof of the house, "broke it up," and let the man down to Jesus' feet through the hole. Such a bold method of bringing someone into God's presence apparently met no objection or resistance. It is easy to see that the Evangelists want us to understand that the restoration of a human being is far more valuable than any material thing, be it the Gadarene swine or the roof of a house.

Note the Lord's immediate response when "He saw their faith." He said, "Son (child), be of good cheer, thy sins be forgiven thee." By far the most important thing for this person, as for anyone else, is to have his sins forgiven. We cannot assume that the Lord had no intention of healing the man physically from the start, even though He told the man, "Arise, take up thy bed," primarily that they might know that He had the power to forgive sins. "Therefore by remitting sins, He did indeed heal man while He also manifested Himself, who He was. For if no one can forgive sins but God alone, while the Lord remitted them and healed men, it is plain that He was Himself the Word of God made the Son of man" (St. Irenaeus, *Against Heresies*, Book 5, ch.17, no. 3).

The Apostles testify to the fact that the first mission of Christ consists of preaching repentance ("Repent, for the kingdom of heaven is at hand") and the forgiveness of sins (Peter and the other apostles, to the high priest, in Acts 5:31). St. Paul, in his sermon in the synagogue at Antioch, says: "Be it known unto you, therefore, men and brethren, that through this man (Jesus Christ) is preached unto you the forgiveness of sins" (Acts 13:38). Later, in his defense before King Agrippa, the Apostle tells the story of his conversion and his commission from the Lord Jesus. Jesus had appeared to him and sent him among the Gentiles "to open their eyes, and to turn them from darkness to light, and from the power of Satan unto God, that they may receive forgiveness of sins, and inheritance among them which are sanctified by faith that is in Me" (Acts 26:18). See also St. Paul's epistles to the Ephesians (1:7) and to the Colossians (1:14): "In whom (Jesus Christ) we have redemption through His blood, the forgiveness of sins."

Still, physical healing was no less a part of the Lord's earthly ministry than the forgiveness of sins, as is evident from the very beginning: "And Jesus went about all Galilee, teaching in their synagogues, and preaching the Gospel of the kingdom, and healing all manner of sickness and all manner of disease among the people" (Matthew 4:23). In many cases, the Lord healed a physical disorder or sickness as a sign of His overall work of restoring the whole man: in curing the physical symptom, He also cures the spiritual cause. St. Ambrose sees in this miracle an image of the resurrection, "since by healing the wounds of soul and body, He forgives the sins of the soul, and He banishes the sickness of the body, which fact means that the whole man has been cured" (*Treatise on the Gospel According to St. Luke*, Book 5, no. 13).

All physical infirmity is ultimately the consequence of sin, in a general sense, and it is impossible to separate healing from forgiveness. Forgiveness, however, remains the priority. Let us seek inner cleansing, the forgiveness of our sins, before we seek healing. And let us bear in mind that, in some cases, the Lord's will for us (and He does have a will for each one who believes in Him) may be to receive forgiveness—and then to give testimony to our faith in Him, while remaining physically crippled by some disease.

5

THE SEVENTH SUNDAY

Two Blind Men and the Demoniac (Matthew 9:27-35)

In the section of St. Matthew's Gospel appointed to be read on the Seventh Sunday after Pentecost (Section 33, or 9:27-35), we find our Lord healing two blind men and a dumb man (a mute) possessed with a devil. Neither St. Luke nor St. Mark relates the first of these miracles, but St. Luke includes the second (11:14-15).

The diseases—blindness and muteness—were physical. The Evangelist does not say what caused the blind men's blindness, the other's inability to speak is clearly attributed to demonic possession.

Physical blindness in the Scriptures often points to a far more serious disease: spiritual blindness. As in the case of other cures, the Lord in one way or another prepared the afflicted for their healing by a kind of spiritual purification. Remember, for example, His first words to the man sick of the palsy: "Son, be of good cheer, thy sins be forgiven thee" (Matthew 9:2). In the present encounter, His question to the blind men, "Believe ye that I am able to do this?" serves as a test, or to bring out the increase of their faith. "Yea, Lord," they answer, indicating that the faith they already had in Him, no doubt because they had heard of Him and His wondrous works, has become more sure. While they at first had addressed Him as "Son of David," they now are able to call Him "Lord." "They call Him no more Son of David, but soar higher, and acknowledge His dominion" (St. John Chrysostom, *On the Gospel According to St. Matthew*, Homily 32, no. 1).

One remarkable detail is that the Lord does not heal them in the presence of the multitude. Instead he leads them into a house to heal them in relative privacy and establish them in that higher level of faith signified by the name "Lord." The point is that He deliberately avoids the praise that the people surely would give Him if He performed the miracle before them. Further, His injunction to them "after their eyes were opened"—"He straightly charged them, See that no man know it"— makes it evident that He sought no glory for what He had done. "He healed within the house and in private, to show us how to avoid vainglory. In everything He did He taught humility"

(Blessed Theophylact, *Explanation of the Holy Gospel According to St. Matthew*, ch. 9, vv. 29-30).

The Evangelist continues: "But they, when they were departed, spread abroad His fame in all that country" (v. 31). Was this behavior blatant disobedience and disregard for the strict command of the One whom they had just acknowledged as Lord? Many modern commentators say yes, but the Fathers of the Church, who had a deeper sense of the Scriptures, a biblical mind, say no. The healed blind men must have understood that the Lord had implied that they could not boast of their healing, as if they were worthy, but were obliged to proclaim God's glory manifest in the miracle. After all, he gave a specific command on another occasion: "Go home to thy friends, and tell them how great things the Lord hath done for thee and hath had compassion on thee" (Mark 5:19; Luke 8:39). St. John Chrysostom says they became "preachers and evangelists" (*On the Gospel According to St. Matthew*, Homily 32).

To return to the blind men's initial plea: we find that "they followed Him, crying and saying, Thou Son of David, have mercy on us." They had no doubt heard of Him. After the raising of Jairus' daughter from the dead—the incident that immediately precedes the present miracle in St. Matthew's Gospel—"the fame hereof went abroad into all that land." Their spiritual blindness was beginning to be healed: they undoubtedly were among those who knew that the Messiah, the Son or descendant of David, was to come. They must have thought that surely the man who did the things that He did must be that Messiah. Even, perhaps, without knowing why, they asked Him for something that God alone can offer: "have mercy on us." Were they asking to be cured of their blindness, or were they already sufficiently illumined to ask for the greater gift, the mercy of God? In any event, two simple words—"Yea, Lord"—show that their faith that He had power to heal had been perfected. "And not merely in works, but also in faith, has God preserved the will of man free and under his own control, saying, 'According to your faith be it unto you.' And again, 'All things are possible to him that believeth' (Mark 9:23); and, 'Go thy way; and as thou hast believed, so be it done unto thee.' (Matthew 8:13) Now all such expressions demonstrate that man is in his own power with respect to faith" (St. Irenaeus, *Against Heresies*, Book 4, ch. 37, no. 5).

Spiritual blindness can be complete or partial. In the heart and mind, one can fail altogether to see God, have no place for Him, and seek the meaning of existence elsewhere. What is perhaps even more common, one can have a tentative belief, somehow believing yet having doubts. We remember the words of the father who asked the Lord to heal his son: "Lord, I believe; help thou mine unbelief" (Mark 9:24). But, when one comes into the presence of Christ, he may reject Him, as many did during our Lord's lifetime, or he may undergo a total conversion. In the same way, a direct experience of the Lord's presence can transform what has been conditional and incomplete into complete faith and trust. Herein we have a deeply personal application of the miracle of the healing of the two blind men.

Now we read in Matthew 9:32: "As they went out, behold, they brought to Him a dumb man possessed with a devil."

This man's affliction is not a natural one; it is neither congenital nor the result of some other disease or accident. Of this we can be sure because the Evangelist relates the muteness to demonic possession. And, as soon as the devil is cast out, the man begins to speak. (See Blessed Theophylact, ibid., vv. 32-33.)

The Lord's fame had spread throughout the land because of His raising Jairus' daughter from the dead (9:26). The number of people who followed Him had increased greatly, and people from among the multitude brought to Him the sick and afflicted. This was the case with the dumb man possessed with a devil. He was brought, and since the devil had bound his tongue, he was unable to call on the Lord. Unlike the blind men, he was unable to ask for healing or mercy. (See St. John Chrysostom, ibid., no. 2.)

What Jesus said or did to cast out the devil is not recorded. Perhaps He said nothing; perhaps He made no gesture. Perhaps He simply willed the cleansing and it was so. There is no indication that the dumb man was anything but passive, but, to be sure, the Lord knew his heart and was moved with compassion because of his affliction. It is also possible that Christ was responding to the intercessory action of those who brought the man to Him. We have seen that He was moved to heal on another occasion "when He saw their faith." We also learn that as soon as the devil was cast out, the man began to speak. None of the Evangelists gives us any notion of what he said.

The crowd that followed the Lord marveled at this sign or miracle. "It was never so seen in Israel," they said, according to St. Matthew. This no doubt means that never before was there such clear evidence of the restoration of a person possessed with a devil. Israel's priests and elders claimed the ability to cast out devils. The evidence of this miracle was too strong to deny, and they were envious.

The Pharisees expressed the displeasure of official religion by making a contradictory accusation: "He casteth out devils through the prince of the devils." St. Matthew does not tell us how the Lord reacted to such an absurd accusation on this occasion, but St. Luke, reporting the same incident, does. On the other hand, St. Matthew records this response in connection with another healing (see 12:25-30), which probably indicates that the Pharisees sought on more than one occasion to discredit or slander the Lord.

As St. Luke's Gospel has it, the Lord said, "Every kingdom divided against itself is brought to desolation, and a house divided against itself falleth. If Satan also be divided against himself, how shall his kingdom stand? because ye say that I cast out devils through Beelzebub. And if I by Beelzebub cast out devils, by whom do your sons cast them out? therefore shall they be your judges" (Luke 11:17-19).

The Lord's response has two purposes: first, it shows how illogical the Pharisee's objection is. Since Satan's purpose is to possess souls and lead them to destruction, it hardly makes sense to invoke him to expel himself from one of his victims. He cannot be expected to participate in the division of his own kingdom. Christ's reference to Satan's kingdom here is very significant: the evil one's kingdom is the great enemy of the kingdom of God made accessible ("at hand") to the human race in the coming of Christ.

Any kingdom, even in the worldly sense, is strong insofar as it is united, but dissensions and in-fighting destroy it. The same is true of "a house" (a people), and here we must conclude that Jesus means the house of Israel. Israel cannot endure precisely because it is divided against itself (and here we have the second purpose of the Lord's response), denying its own purpose and destiny by rejecting the Savior promised by the law and the prophets. For St. Ambrose, the Lord's response applies not only to Israel but also to heretics and schismatics, who at the prompting of the unclean spirit, the devil, attempt to set up a kingdom apart from the indivisible, true kingdom, which is Christ's Church (*Treatise on the Gospel According to St. Luke*, Book 7, nos. 91-95).

Finally, the Lord had given power and authority to His own apostles to cast out devils (Matthew 10:1; Mark 3:15, etc.), and it is clear that they exercised this power (Luke 10:17). They were indeed sons of Israel, and it is to them that the Lord makes reference when He asks, "By whom do your sons cast out devils?" (Luke 11:19). It was from Him that their authority came, and yet they had not been accused of invoking the name of Beelzebub, the prince of devils, to cast out devils. Why, indeed, would they accuse the One who was the very source of this power and not the ones empowered? Their sons, then, are the witnesses that already, by their actions, pass judgment on the Christ-destroying religious leaders.

6

THE EIGHTH SUNDAY

Feeding the Five Thousand (Matthew 14:14-22)

When the holy Prophet and Forerunner John the Baptist was beheaded, his disciples "took up the body, and buried it, and went and told Jesus." Although Christ, as God, already knew of His forerunner's tragic end, He received the news as any man would have, not being willing yet to reveal His identity fully. And, because Jesus' signs and wonders had led Herod to believe that He was John the Baptist risen from the dead, the Lord elected to go away rather than to expose Himself to danger before the appointed time for His suffering and death.

He went by boat to a desert place, apparently wanting to get away from the crowds. But "when the people had heard (of His departure), they followed Him on foot out of the cities." In other words, they went around the lake to reach the other side before Him. Now the Lord, who is full of mercy, saw the faith of the people who followed Him without provisions. He "was moved with compassion toward them, and He healed their sick" (Matthew 14:12-14).

The multitude included John's disciples. Now that their master was dead, they attached themselves closely to Jesus, no doubt remembering John's own declaration that Jesus was mightier than he (Matthew 3:11) and that Jesus was to increase while he was to decrease (John 3:30). John's work of preparing the way was finished, and now the One whom he had proclaimed had come.

The "desert place" to which Jesus retreated becomes the scene of an extraordinary miracle that is not only a further demonstration of the Lord's compassion but also one that teaches a number of doctrinal and spiritual lessons. (The miracle is recorded by all four Evangelists, and St. Matthew's account [14:15-21] forms the Gospel reading for the Eighth Sunday after Pentecost; see, in the other Gospels, Luke 9:12-17; Mark 6:35-44; and John 6:1-14.)

We have noted that it was compassion that moved the Lord to heal the sick from among the multitude that followed Him. Now, although fully aware that the people, in their zeal to hear Him, have neglected to bring food, He does not simply decide to feed them. He waits for His disciples to take the initiative. They come to Him and ask to be sent off to find food in the nearby villages. His response must have come as a surprise: "They need not depart; give ye them to eat." They had approached the One whom they called Master but One whom they still knew only as a man, albeit One who was a prophet and teacher. They could hardly have yet imagined a miraculous feeding. They meet the Lord's response with an objection: they have but five loaves and two fishes (v. 17).

It is evident that the Lord wants to see in His disciples some concern for the people's good, in some way learning from Him and imitating Him and His own compassion for mankind. They do not disappoint Him. As on other occasions when the Lord has done miraculous works, He is moved by the intercessory action of others. Christ Himself will feed the multitude, but, very significantly, he will use the disciples to carry out His will. Clearly, Christ's plan for His work includes human instruments who act, not as mediators, but as ministers of His design.

The faith of the disciples and of the people was great but not yet perfected. They did not yet fully understand who He was. Had they been convinced at this time that He was God, the Son of God, by whom and through whom all things were created (Hebrews 1:2; 1 Corinthians 8:6; John 1:3), who, in His providence, feeds the whole world, they would have known that He had the power to feed the crowd.

The Fathers of the Church find significance in every detail of what follows. "Neither the number, the order, nor what is left over after the people had eaten is insignificant" (St. Ambrose, *Treatise on the Gospel According to St. Luke*, Book 6, no. 79).

Someone—"a lad," according to St. John—had brought five loaves and two fishes. His willingness to share so little says a great deal about the atmosphere of faith and love that the Lord's presence brought. It also teaches us to share even when there is no abundance. Sometimes we are willing to share only when we have too much for ourselves.

Some ancient commentators (the Blessed Theophylact, for example, in his *Explanation of the Holy Gospel According to St. Matthew*, 14:17-19) see the Lord's command to sit and the people's obedience as a lesson in the significance of food. One eats to live; that is, he takes what is necessary to sustain life. The follower of Christ should not make eating an elaborate affair or give great attention to presumably suitable settings. Food should be simple. Thus the Lord multiplied only the simple provisions that were already at hand: barley bread (common among the poor) and fish. Further, no matter how simple and scarce the fare, before touching any food, the Christian always remembers to give thanks to Him who gives all food (St.

John Chrysostom, *On the Gospel According to St. Matthew*, Homily 49, no. 2). This the Lord indicates by looking up to heaven (v. 19).

He "blessed and broke the bread" as was the custom among the Jews. Then "He gave the loaves to the disciples and the disciples to the multitude." The bread multiplied in their hands, and again we see the Lord's plan at work: to make use of His chosen servants to minister to the rest.

The Fathers were sensitive to the numbers brought to our attention in Scripture. This number consciousness was familiar to the Jews, and no doubt the early Christians understood such symbolism as well. For some of the Fathers, the five loaves represent the five senses, which need healing because of the sinfulness in which the senses play a part. Others say the number five represents the first five books of the Bible, and the two fishes represent the New Testament, consisting of the Gospels and epistles. In any event, we must respect the fact that numbers such as these were fixed in the minds of the early Christians and the Fathers, and we often see the influence of this consciousness in the life of the Church. We have always used five loaves in the eucharist, which is, of course, the means by which every generation of Christians has been miraculously fed, spiritually nourished. The fish became a secret sign, the drawing of which was a means for Christians to identify themselves to one another in the early days of the Church. It happens that the initial and final letters of the Greek words for *fish* and for *Jesus* are the same.

Concerning the feeding of more than five thousand people, the Blessed Theophylact has this to say: "Jesus withdrew to a desert place, to the nations who were desolate without God, and He healed the sick in soul and then He fed them. For if He had not forgiven our sins and healed our sicknesses by baptism He could not have nourished us by giving us the immaculate

Mysteries, for no one partakes of Holy Communion who has not first been baptized." For this holy Father, the healing of "their sick" and the miraculous feeding are figures of the two primary holy mysteries (*Explanation of the Holy Gospel According to St. Matthew*, ch. 14:14-21). St. Ambrose of Milan likewise sees in this miracle a figure of the eucharist: "Here there is also a mystery in the fact that the people eat and are satisfied and that the Apostles serve them. For this being filled indicates that hunger has forever disappeared, since there will be no more hunger once the food of Christ is received. And the service of the Apostles makes us foresee their distributing (in communion) the Body and Blood of the Lord" (*Treatise on the Gospel According to St. Luke*, Book 6, no. 84). The service of the holy Apostles in relation to this miracle is not only a figure of their continued service as ministers of the holy mysteries but also of the service of their successors, as one other important detail in the story will show.

The fragments that remained were gathered up by the Apostles; there was so much that they were able to fill twelve baskets, corresponding to the number of the Apostles. They were thus commissioned to continue to feed the hungry, but only later would they understand the full extent of this commission. Several Fathers (such as St. John Chrysostom, *On the Gospel According to St. Matthew*, Homily 49, no. 3) note that it was the fragments of what had been given to the multitude and not new, untouched breads. In this way, they were being prepared to continue the same miracle in the days that followed, and to understand the significance of the miracle when they would be commissioned to distribute the bread of heaven and the chalice of salvation.

In the Holy Gospel According to St. John (ch. 6), the feeding of the five thousand and the Lord's walking on the sea are followed by His discourse on Himself as the Bread of Life.

The people who have eaten and been filled are ready to believe on Him, but not according to His will. He knows that they are concerned only about their material welfare. In fact, He knows that "they would come and take Him by force, to make Him a king" (John 6:15). Their motive for seeking Him He clearly understands, and He tells them that it is not because they have seen and understood the sign, but because they have been fed (John 6:26). And then, to make it clear that the miraculous feeding signified something greater than a response to their physical needs, He says: "Labor not for the meat which perisheth, but for the meat which endureth unto everlasting life, which the Son of Man will give unto you" (John 6:27). When they were requesting a sign so that they might believe in Him, they recalled the miracle of the feeding of their forefathers in the desert with manna from heaven (Exodus 16). Yet that miracle was not enough to cause their forefathers to follow the law of God and to obey His commandments. Jesus declares Himself to be the True Bread from heaven given to them by the Father, and thus the manna in the desert and the bread of this miracle are both signs of that True Bread. But those who have received the miraculous feeding in the "desert place" are in danger of the same misunderstanding as their forefathers. To have everlasting life, they must believe on Him; to hunger no more, they must receive and partake of the True Bread. (See St. Augustine, *Tractate 25 on the Gospel According to St. John*, no. 10)

In response to the Jews' question, "How can this man give us His flesh to eat?" (v. 52), Jesus utters His "hard saying" (v. 60): "Verily, verily, I say unto you, Except ye eat the flesh of the Son of Man, and drink His blood, ye have no life in you" (vv. 53-58). It was because of this that "many of His disciples went back, and walked no more with Him" (v. 66). The Fathers (such as St. Cyril of Jerusalem, *Catechetical Lectures* 22, nos. 1-4) consistently understand His sayings here as referring not only to complete faith and trust in Him but also to the holy Eucharist, at whose institution He said: "Take, eat, this is my body" and "drink ye all of this, this is my blood." We shall have the opportunity to explore this discourse later when we study the signs in St. John's Gospel.

7

THE NINTH SUNDAY

The Lord Walks on the Sea (Matthew 14:22-34)

The Apostles' proclamation of Christ after the descent of the Spirit at Pentecost included specific references to His miracles. St. Peter spoke of "Jesus of Nazareth, a man approved (attested to) of God among you by miracles and wonders and signs" (Acts 2:22). These signs and wonders are an essential part of the preaching of Christ the Redeemer, for they not only demonstrate His love and compassion for suffering mankind but they prove beyond doubt that He is what He claimed to be, the Son of God and God incarnate.

Any preaching of Christ that leaves out His miracles makes for a defective, distorted picture of His saving work. It is lamentable that many unorthodox evangelists and preachers in our own time, attempting to adjust Jesus Christ to modern likes and dislikes, either ignore the miraculous content of the Gospel or write it off as symbolic. For Rudolf Bultmann, a twentieth-century German New Testament scholar, the miracles are generally a part of the mythological language and framework that the New Testament employs to convey the truth; although they contain elements of truth, they are not the real message, and they are not historically true. Bultmann's method of understanding Scripture and the work of Christ included what has come to be called "demythologization."

Among the miracles that especially prove Jesus to be God incarnate are those that demonstrate His power over creation. He, the very Creator of the physical world and the Designer of the natural order, obviously can suspend or alter that order if He wills to do so. "Whatsoever the Lord willed, that did He in heaven, and in earth, in the seas, and the deeps" (Psalm 134/135:6).

The miracle recorded in Matthew 14:22-34 (Mark 6:45-54; John 6:15-21), and recounted in the Divine Liturgy on the Ninth Sunday after Pentecost, is an example of this kind. Others include the stilling of the tempest (Matthew 8:23-27; Mark 4:35-41; Luke 8:22-25), the miraculous catch of fish (Matthew 4:18-22; Mark 1:16-20; Luke 5:1-11; John 1:35-43), and the withering of the fig tree (Matthew 21:19).

The miracle of Jesus' walking on the sea is perhaps the best known of all. It is reported not only in Matthew but also in John 6 and Mark 6 soon after the feeding of the five thousand. We see Jesus commanding His disciples to board a boat and row across the sea, while He remains behind to send the multitude away. Then He goes up alone to a hill to pray.

Meanwhile, because of a contrary wind, the ship in the midst of the sea is tossed about by the waves and the disciples are afraid. "And in the fourth watch of the night Jesus went unto them, walking on the sea. And when the disciples saw Him walking on the sea, they were troubled, saying, It is a spirit; and they cried out for fear. But straightway Jesus spake unto them, Be of good cheer; it is I; be not afraid. And Peter answered Him and said, Lord, if it be thou, bid me come to thee on the water. And He said, Come. And when Peter was come down out of the ship, he walked on the water, to go to Jesus. But when he saw the wind boisterous, he was afraid; and beginning to sink, he cried, saying, Lord, save me. And immediately Jesus stretched forth His hand, and caught him, and said unto him, O thou of little faith, wherefore didst thou doubt?

And when they were come into the ship, the wind ceased. Then they that were in the ship came and worshipped Him, saying, Of a truth thou art the Son of God" (Matthew 14:25-33).

Jesus' demonstration of His power over creation—His walking on the water, His saving Peter, and His causing the wind to cease—leads the disciples to recognize and confess His divinity.

The Blessed Theophylact, in his commentary on St. Matthew, opens up the miracle's spiritual meaning: "The boat is the earth; the waves, man's life that is troubled by evil spirits; the night is ignorance. In the fourth watch, that is, at the end of the ages, Christ appeared. The first watch was the covenant with Abraham; the second, the law of Moses; the third, the prophets; and the fourth, the coming of Christ. For He saved those who were drowning when He came and was with us so that we might know and worship Him as God. See also how Peter's later denial, return and repentance were prefigured by what happened to him here on the sea" (*Explanation of the Holy Gospel According to St. Matthew*, ch. 14).

St. John Chrysostom (*On the Gospel According to St. Matthew*, Homily 50, no. 1) makes particularly striking observations that can help and comfort, as well as admonish, today's Christians in their spiritual struggle. Christ, he points out, not only knew beforehand the disciples' fear and the danger they were in, but even permitted them to be tossed about for most of the night. Although they had already seen Him calm a storm and save them from peril (Matthew 8:23-27), now their fear was so great that they did not remember Him to put their hope in Him. So it is with us. We know that Christ is the Lord. We know that He can deliver us from tribulation and perhaps have seen Him do so on other occasions. But when we experience great troubles, attacks of the devil and temptations, we forget Him and His saving power and are overcome by fear. He delays coming to us when we fail to call on Him or put our trust in Him, even allowing us to be tested. He still comes to us, however. Even then we fail to recognize him, just like the disciples in the boat. It is then that we hear Him saying, "Be of good cheer, it is I; be not afraid." Like the disciples, we have to be reminded, because of our little faith, that He always lifts us up and puts out His hand to rescue us.

8

THE TENTH SUNDAY

The Cure of the Epileptic (Matthew 17:14-23)
St. Matthew 17:14-23, appointed to be read on the Tenth Sunday after Pentecost, describes the healing of a young man brought to the Lord by his father. (St. Mark 9:16-30 offers a longer account; St. Luke 9:38-42 offers a shorter one.) The son's condition is characterized by St. Matthew as that of a "lunatic," by St. Mark as possession by a "dumb spirit," and by St. Luke as being taken "by a spirit."

The healing is summarized very simply: "And Jesus rebuked the devil, and he departed out of him" (Matthew 17:18). "He rebuked the foul spirit, saying unto him, Thou dumb and deaf spirit, I charge thee, come out of him, and enter no more into him" (Mark 9:25). "And Jesus rebuked the unclean spirit, and healed the child, and delivered him again to his father" (Luke 9:42). All three accounts make it clear that the Lord treats this as a case of demon possession, not as a physical sickness. He "rebukes"—reprimands, accuses and stops the evil work of—the demon, so that he may know that he has been discovered.

What is particularly striking in these narratives is how the Lord responds to the child's father, the multitude, and finally His disciples. The father says to Jesus, "I brought him to thy disciples, and they could not cure him" (Matthew 17:16). All three Evangelists record the allegation in practically the same terms. Likewise Jesus' answer: "O faithless and perverse generation, how long shall I be with you? how long shall I suffer you?" (v. 17).

At first sight, one might conclude that the Lord's reprimand is directed to the disciples, but we must consider that "when He came to His disciples, He saw a great multitude about them, and the scribes questioning with them" (Mark 9:14). In other words, this event took place in the presence of that multitude, and it was in response to Jesus' asking the scribes, "What question ye with them?" that the lunatic's father came forth from the multitude and related that the disciples were unable to cure him.

The fact that the Lord accused a "generation" of being faithless and perverse leads us to believe that those strong words were addressed primarily to the scribes and, generally, to the whole Jewish people, represented by the great crowd. Admittedly, the disciples were weak in faith, too. The Lord will tell them so subsequently. It is only after the crucifixion and the resurrection that they are perfected in faith. It also appears that the three disciples who had witnessed the transfiguration (referred to as "pillars" in Galatians 2:9) were not among the disciples being questioned by the scribes (St. John Chrysostom, *On the Gospel According to St. Matthew*, Homily 57, no. 3).

Alone with Jesus, the disciples ask why they could not cast out the demon (Matthew 17:19). They seem to have come to doubt the power that He had given them (Matthew 10:1). In this privacy, Jesus reproaches them for their unbelief. Even if their faith were no greater than a mustard seed, He says, nothing would be impossible for them.

The child's father is also reproached for his lack of faith. Several of the Fathers address his complaint against the Apos-

tles with severity. For example, St. Cyril of Alexandria (op.
cit., Homily 52) directs this rebuke to the father: "And yet it
was owing to thy own want of faith that the grace availed not.
Dost thou not perceive that thou wast thyself the cause that the
child was not delivered from his severe illness?" He goes on to
say: "He who says that those (disciples) were powerless for the
expulsion of evil spirits, who by Christ's will had received
power to cast them (the devils) out, finds fault with the grace
itself rather than the receivers of it... It is plain, therefore, in
every way that the man wickedly found fault with Christ's
power in saying of the holy Apostles, 'They could not cast it
out.'"

The father's plea, as reported by St. Mark, reflects uncer-
tainty: "If thou canst do anything, have compassion on us, and
help us" (9:22). The Lord turns the expression back to him: "If
thou canst believe..." (9:23). This prompts the desperate father
to take his first steps toward faith. He "cried out, and said with
tears, Lord, I believe; help thou mine unbelief" (9:24). The beginning of this man's faith and his humble prayer for deeper
faith make him a model for those of us who realize how little
faith we have and sincerely wish to see it increased.

Finally, the Lord tells those whom He had chosen and
given power to cast out demons and heal all manner of disease
(Matthew 10:1) what they needed to make use of that gift.
"Howbeit this kind goeth not out but by prayer and fasting"
(Matthew 17:21). Their faith will be completed by two vitally
important works: they must pray and they must fast. Prayer is
faith in action, and fasting is an essential aid to prayer. Undoubtedly the Lord is telling them and us that recourse to
prayer and fasting is not to be had only in curing demon possession. These disciplines constitute the foundation of the
spiritual life. As the Lord makes clear by pairing them, they
are inseparable.

One of the most common self-deceptions among Christians today is that prayer is essential but fasting is optional. Too often we hear jokes about the ways in which we avoid fasting, but even more often we attempt to justify our failure. Let us learn from this miracle that we must believe with all our heart and mind, and that that faith must be built up by prayer and fasting. Both are signs of the complete transformation that must be the goal of Christian life. And they help us to that end.

9

THE SEVENTEENTH SUNDAY

The Woman of Canaan's Daughter (Matthew 15:21-28)

The reading from the Holy Gospel for the Seventeenth Sunday after Pentecost (Matthew 15:21-28; see also Mark 7:24-30) presents a picture of an extraordinary woman whose daughter was demon-possessed. She is described as "a woman from Canaan" (Matthew 15:22) or as "a Greek, a Syro-Phoenician by nation" (Mark 7:26), a descendant of the original inhabitants of Canaan.

The mention of Canaan brings to mind the wickedness and corruption attributed to its early inhabitants. The Jews were to shun them (Genesis 13:13; Leviticus 18:27). It must have seemed to the Apostles the least likely place to initiate the "call of the Gentiles."

According to both St. Matthew and St. Mark, just before He met the woman from Canaan, the Lord answered the accusation of the Pharisees and scribes against His disciples. They had sharply criticized Jesus' followers for not observing "the tradition of the elders," particularly with regard to eating and certain ritual requirements. But the Lord pointed out that the Jews were far guiltier. They failed to keep the commandments of God. They took deep offense at His judgment, which was an echo of

Isaiah the Prophet: "This people honoureth me with their lips, but their heart is far from me" (Matthew 15:8, 12; see Isaiah 29:13). The Lord summarized His teaching for His disciples and everyone else who witnessed this discussion: "There is nothing from without (outside of) a man, that entering into him can defile him: but the things which come out of him, those are they that defile the man" (Mark 7:15; Matthew 15:17-20).

Rejected by His own people, Jesus went "unto the borders of Tyre and Sidon," the land of the Gentiles, and would have hid Himself. Then the woman of Canaan "came out of the same coasts and cried unto Him, saying, Have mercy on me, O Lord, thou Son of David; my daughter is grievously vexed with a devil" (Matthew 15:22).

She had heard of Him, and, although one might not suppose that she would be familiar with Israel's expectations concerning the Messiah, her plea for mercy and her addressing Him as "Lord" and "Son of David" lead us to think otherwise. She appears to have known who He was.

The scene of her encounter with the Lord merits special attention. Her bold approach, on the borders of her own land, was a dangerous undertaking. Note also that the Lord went to the very place He had forbidden His disciples to go—"Go not into the way of the Gentiles" (Matthew 10:5). The woman's desperation over her daughter and her perception of Christ overcame whatever fears she might have had. The Lord, on the other hand, was not bound by the prohibition He issued to the disciples. Furthermore, He had not gone to the Gentiles specifically to preach the Good News. Obviously, as the all-knowing God, He already knew both the woman and what was going to happen.

What follows her initial plea is remarkable, first because "He answered her not a word" (Matthew 15:23). While He obviously knew her profound humility and her faith, it seems to have been His purpose to allow her to manifest these virtues, or, as some have thought, even to test her faith. The disciples' request, "Send her away; for she crieth after us," shows not only their annoyance but also their misunderstanding of the Lord's purpose. Apparently they wanted Him to grant her request so that she might go away, since He had declared that He was "not sent but unto the lost sheep of Israel."

The woman's first plea—"Have mercy on me"—and her second, in the face of His silence—"Help me"—might lead some people to think that she was more concerned for herself than for her daughter. But the Lord perceived that she so loved her daughter that she could identify the latter's suffering with her own. "She worshipped Him," it is said, and it was then that Christ said what could have been terribly offensive to her: "It is not meet to take the children's bread, and cast it to dogs." He was saying that His beneficence was intended for those whom He first called "sheep" but now "children." Actually, He even softened His reference to her and her kind: the Greek word translated "dog" is actually "puppy" or "pet," a domesticated and loved animal. Nevertheless, He seems to have made the silence of His first rejection more intense by His answer. Her extreme humility becomes manifest with her reply: "Truth, Lord: yet the dogs eat of the crumbs that fall from their masters' table." Not only is she willing to accept, because of her unworthiness, only a small part of what is intended for the Hebrews but now she even calls them her "masters." He grants her request: "O woman, great is thy faith: be it unto thee even as thou wilt." St. Athanasius comments: "Now that she was hitherto an unbeliever, one of the profane, He shows, saying, 'It is not meet to take the children's bread, and to cast it to dogs.' She then, being convinced by the power of the Word, and having changed her ways, also gained faith; for the Lord no longer spoke to her as a dog, but conversed with her as a human being, saying, 'O woman, great is thy faith'" ("Paschal Letter 7," no. 7). St. Justin Martyr concludes that even for a descendant of the Canaanites, "who has faith and recognizes the truth of His own words," the curse of being a servant is removed ("Dialogue with Trypho," ch. 139).

The Canaanite woman's plea is offered to us as an example in the Great Canon of St. Andrew: "Be not overcome by despair, my soul; for thou hast heard of the faith of the woman of Canaan, and how through it her daughter was healed by the word of God. Cry out from the depth of thy heart, 'Save me also, Son of David,' as she once cried to Christ" (Wednesday of the First Week of the Great Fast, Ode 9).

The most important lesson for those of us in the midst of our spiritual struggle is this: we must never approach the Lord with the sense that we are worthy of what we ask for. Sometimes pride, self-love, and self-confidence bring us to this point. Also, we easily despair in our own prayers, even when we spend very little time in praying, and tend to leave it to others to pray for us. Intercession is a most desirable part of our prayer life, and we should always pray for others and ask them to pray for us. Note what St. John Chrysostom says about this application of the narrative: "Mark thou, I pray thee, how when the Apostles had failed, and had not succeeded, this woman had success. So great a thing is assiduity (diligence and perseverance) in prayer. Yea, He had even rather be solicited by us, guilty as we are, for those who belong to us, than by others on our behalf" (*On the Gospel According to St. Matthew*, Homily 52).

10

THE EIGHTEENTH SUNDAY

The Great Catch of Fish (Luke 5:1-11)

The Gospel lesson for the Eighteenth Sunday after Pentecost—St. Luke 5:1-11—recounts the miraculous catch of fish, another sign pointing to the Lord's power over all creation. The story is remarkable, not least because of what it says about the reaction of those who were to become His Apostles, especially Peter. The miracle belongs to the Lord's early ministry, just before He calls the twelve from among the larger crowd that has begun to follow Him (6:13-16). On this occasion, He appears to have singled out three—Peter, James, and John—for a special role. They, before the others, become eyewitnesses to His power and divinity.

The scene is the Lake of Gennesaret, along whose shores were the cities and towns where Jesus would do so much of His work. The number of the people who were following Him had increased, and they were eager to hear the word of God (5:1). There were two ships standing by the shore, and Jesus boarded one of them, Simon's, and asked him to move it out a short distance from the land so that He could teach the people from there. When He finished speaking, He told Simon Peter, "Launch out into the deep, and let down your nets for a draught" (5:4). Experienced fishermen, they were convinced that it would be useless to try any further. Simon, as their spokesman, answered Him, "Master, we have toiled all the night, and have taken nothing." But then Simon added, in an expression of complete trust and obedience, "nevertheless at thy word I will let down the net" (5:5).

Thus, in spite of all their expertise in their trade, which told them that "the fish were not biting," their trust in Him, whom they had become convinced was the Messiah of Israel, was such that they were willing to put aside their own experience and mastery in order to conform to His will. Simon Peter's declaration, which, of course, was made in the name of James and John as well, is one of the most perfect expressions of conformity with the will of God recorded in Holy Scripture. It recalls that other response, that of the Mother of God, which indicated that, in spite of the human impossibility of her bearing a child, and of her knowing or foreseeing all that she would suffer because of it, she was willing to conform to God's holy will. "How shall this be, seeing I know not a man?... Behold the handmaid of the Lord; be it unto me according to thy word" (Luke 1:34, 38).

The launching out into the deep has been interpreted in several ways by the Fathers. One says that it was the Lord's will that His disciples, who were to be "fishers of men," were to go beyond what was familiar, to lesser-known, far-away, perhaps dangerous places. He was preparing them for the future when He would show them where they should go to preach the Gospel. Here, we could understand that it was not only to the familiar people, the Jews, but also to those Gentiles who would also be brought into the Church. (See Blessed Theophylact, *Explanation of the Holy Gospel According to St. Luke*, ch. 5.) Another says that the Apostles, in their future evangelization, were to plunge into the midst of the world of controversies, to deal with its problems and needs, facing all its dangers and its oppositions. (See St. Ambrose, *Treatise on the Gospel According to St. Luke*, Book 4, no. 71).

The catch itself may well be understood as a figure of the Church and its mission to bring in all peoples. As fishers of men, they would have the duty to carry the Gospel to everyone, the good and the bad, and to extend the kingdom of God on earth. We recall the parable of the Marriage Feast of the King's Son, to which the Lord likens the kingdom of heaven, wherein we see that the servants of the king were obliged, when they were sent out the third time, to bring in as many as they could find, both bad and good. The bad, to be sure, are not blessed to continue to be bad. With the grace of the Holy Spirit and by their response to it, they will be transformed and made fit to participate in the wedding feast: we remember that one of the guests dared to present himself at the feast without a wedding garment, that is, without the necessary preparation and repentance (see Matthew 22:2-14). Finally, we might add that it would not be difficult to find some analogies in the Church's history with the net's breaking, but this subject is too complex and might appear too contrived for us to deal with it here.

What is truly remarkable is Simon Peter's reaction to this happening: "When Simon Peter saw it, he fell down at Jesus' knees, saying, Depart from me; for I am a sinful man, O Lord. For he was astonished, and all that were with him, at the draught of the fishes which they had taken: and so also was James, and John, the sons of Zebedee, which were partners with Simon" (5:8-10).

We might have expected St. Peter to be overjoyed at the enormous catch. The time for fishing is normally the night, but here, during the day, he had had perhaps the greatest catch of his whole career. And yet his response to what was at once a demonstration of the Lord's unlimited dominion over creation and a great kindness to him and to his partners, was a sudden and deep sense of his own sinfulness. "Peter, carried back to the memory of his former sins, trembles and is afraid, and as being impure ventures not to receive Him Who is pure; and his fear was laudable, for he had been taught by the Law to distinguish between the holy and the profane" (St. Cyril of Alexandria, *Commentary on the Gospel of St. Luke*, ch. 5, v. 8). His humility—the sense that he is unworthy to be in the presence of such holiness, in the presence of God Himself—prompted his exclamation: "Depart from me." He could not endure to stand so near to the divine majesty, for what he immediately recognized was who Jesus really was. We note, by the way, that when he told Jesus that they had worked all the night without success, he called Him "Master," but now he changes and calls Him "Lord." Also, he must have perceived at that moment a truth about which St. Paul would write later to the Romans: "the goodness of God leadeth thee to repentance" (2:4).

The Lord's response to Peter's act of extreme contrition, "Fear not," was not only comforting but also indicative of a new and enduring relationship with Him. This was made clear in what the Lord said immediately after: "from henceforth thou shalt catch men." The word translated as "catch" means literally "capture" or "take alive" and is not the usual word for catch, which Peter had used in verse 5. This is understood to refer to the conversion of men and women, through the preaching of the Gospel, and their being brought into the Church.

"And when they had brought their ships to land, they forsook all and followed Him" (v. 11). Whether, on this occasion, the Lord said to them, "Follow me," as He is quoted in Matthew 4:19 and Mark 1:17, the fact is that they did leave everything behind and follow Him. It matters little that His call "to catch men" was addressed to Peter alone in St. Luke's Gospel, since in both of the other two Gospels, He says to Peter and to his brother, Andrew, "I will make you fishers of men."

Thus, we learn from this miracle, as did those disciples, about the Lord Himself, His Person, power, and authority. Such is the nature of Christ's miracles. We also learn much about what our relation to Him must be.

Having put our whole trust in Christ, knowing of His unbounded love for us, and that He desires only our salvation, we must be ready always to obey His will. This we must do even if our experience or any other human consideration might tell us that what we perceive to be His will is not practical. We have seen how Peter overcame this temptation. People often ask how they are to know God's will for them. Glib answers such as "Oh, you will know" are unhelpful and misleading. It is not so simple as some imagine; we must actively seek to know the will of God. St. Paul speaks of "understanding what the will of the Lord is" (Ephesians 5:17). This we earnestly and persistently ask for primarily in prayer. Following the Apostle, we may also ask others to pray for us specifically for this purpose (Colossians 1:9).

St. Ambrose emphasizes that we must learn from St. Peter to confess our own unworthiness to be in the presence of the Lord. "You must also say, 'Depart from me, for I am a sinful man, O Lord,' so that the Lord may respond to you, 'Fear not.' Confess your sins to the Lord, for He forgives. Do not be afraid of giving the Lord what is yours, since He granted to you what is His" (*Treatise on the Gospel According to St. Luke*, Book 4, no. 79). In becoming man, the Son of God has given to men the power to become the sons of God (John 1:12) and to participate in the divine nature (2 Peter 1:4), in the divine life.

Peter, Andrew, James, and John forsook all and followed Him. Peter and Andrew, according to Matthew 4:20 and Mark 1:18, left their nets; that is, their occupation. James and John left both their ship and their father: their jobs and family, in other words (Matthew 4:22; Mark 1:20). Later, Peter, in the name of all the disciples, will say: "Behold, we have forsaken all, and followed thee" (Matthew 19:27). And the Lord will say, extending His promise beyond the small group of disciples: "Every one that hath forsaken house, or brethren, or sisters, or father, or mother, or wife, or children, or lands, for my sake, shall receive an hundredfold, and shall inherit everlasting life" (Matthew 19:29). Simple abandonment of family or responsibility does not of itself gain one's salvation. When the Lord says, "for my name's sake," He is saying that if any one or any thing is more precious to a person than the Lord Himself, if those things and persons are obstacles to following and serving Him, then they must be abandoned. (See the Blessed Theophylact, *Explanation of the Holy Gospel According to St. Matthew*, ch. 19, v. 29).

11

THE TWENTIETH SUNDAY

The Son of the Widow of Nain (Luke 7:11-16)

The liturgical texts for Lazarus Saturday testify to the resurrection of Lazarus as "an assurance of the general resurrection" (as the Troparion puts it) and "of the deliverance of all men from corruption" (Matins, Praises). Repeatedly we find similar expressions in the writings of the Fathers.

The Gospels report two additional resurrections (other than the Lord's own), and Fathers such as St. Cyril of Alexandria and St. Ambrose of Milan see those, too, as pledges and figures of the resurrection of all at the end of the world. These are the raising of Jairus' daughter and the raising of the son of the widow of Nain. The latter is the subject of the Gospel section for the Twentieth Sunday after Pentecost (Luke 7:11-16).

"Now when He came nigh to the gate of the city, behold, there was a dead man carried out, the only son of his mother, and she was a widow: and much people of the city was with her" (v. 12). The Evangelist says nothing about the Lord's intent in going to Nain. He undoubtedly foresaw the meeting with this funeral procession, but it is evident that He did not enter the city in response to anyone's seeking His intervention. We may compare these circumstances with those surrounding the other resurrections. In Luke 8 we will find that the father of a young girl "who lay a-dying" purposely sought the Lord's help. In the case of Lazarus, Jesus received word from the sisters, Mary and Martha, that their brother was sick (John 11:3). The three circumstances are different: Lazarus was the Lord's friend. Grief—the sisters' and His own—moved Jesus to restore him to life. Jairus interceded for his own daughter, but no one spoke to the Lord about the widow's son. In each case Christ, the Lord of life, showed the same compassion for suffering humanity.

It has been pointed out that these three resurrections cover the "three successive aspects of death": Jairus' daughter still lay in the bed where she died; the widow's son was being carried to his burial; Lazarus was dead four days, and his body had begun to decompose (see *The Year of Grace of the Lord*, by a Monk of the Eastern Church, p. 22). The power of Christ, who is the Life and the Lord of life, to restore anyone among the dead, no matter the time or circumstance, is clearly manifested.

The story of Lazarus, especially, teaches us that the Lord was full of compassion in the face of human tragedy. What powerful witness to His human nature does that briefest of verses bear: "Jesus wept" (John 11:35; see St. John Chrysostom, *On the Gospel According to St. John*, Homily 62). So it was in the meeting with the widow of Nain. "And when the Lord saw her, He had compassion on her, and said unto her, Weep not. And he came and touched the bier; and they that bare him stood still. And He said, young man, I say unto thee, Arise" (vv. 13-14). We can only imagine the woman's reaction in that fleeting moment between "Weep not" and "Arise." The power of Jesus' word stopped everything—her weeping and the procession of the bier.

Weep not. The very words give assurance that the Lord will remove the cause of weeping. No one protests or jeers as did some before the other resurrections. When Jesus told the mourners in Jairus' house, "Weep not, she is not dead, but sleepeth, they laughed Him to scorn, knowing that she was dead" (Luke 8:52-53). Lazarus' sisters showed faith, but when He told them to open the grave, Martha must have felt it was useless. "Lord, by this time he stinketh; for he hath been dead four days," she said (John 11:39).

At the Lord's command to the widow's son, "he that was dead sat up, and began to speak. And he delivered him to his mother" (v. 15). St. Cyril of Alexandria notes well the details:

"Observe here too, I pray you, the accuracy of the expression; for the divine Evangelist not only says that the dead man sat up, but lest anyone should by false arguments attack the miracle, saying, 'What wonder! if by means of some artifice or other the body was set upright! for it is not yet clearly proved to be alive, or delivered from the bonds of death'—for this reason he very skillfully notes down two proofs one after the other, sufficient to produce the conviction that he did in very truth arise and was restored. 'For he began,' he says, 'to speak'—but an inanimate body cannot speak. And 'He gave him to his mother'—but assuredly the woman would not have taken her son back to her house if he had been dead, and had breathed his last" (*Commentary on the Gospel of St. Luke*, Homily 36).

For this same saint, one of the most important details is that Jesus "came and touched the bier" (v. 14). "What is more powerful than the Word of God? Why then did He not effect the miracle by a word only, but also touched the bier? It was, my beloved, that thou mightest learn that the holy body of Christ is effectual for the salvation of man. For the flesh of the Almighty Word is the body of life, and was clothed with His might. For consider, that iron, when brought into contact with fire, produces the effects of fire, and fulfills its functions; so, because it became the flesh of the Word, who gives life to all, it therefore also has the power of giving life, and annihilates the influence of death and corruption. May our Lord Jesus Christ also touch us, that delivering us from evil works, even from fleshly lusts, He may unite us to the assemblies of the saints" (ibid.).

These three resurrections in the Gospels make it clear that the Lord is moved by His divine love and compassion to heal and restore life. But we see also the depth, the completeness of His taking upon Himself our fallen nature, when as a Man He is filled with compassion for loved ones and their sadness in the face of the tragedy that is death.

12

THE TWENTY-FOURTH SUNDAY

Jairus' Daughter and the Woman with an Issue of Blood
(Luke 8:41-56)

Let us return to the raising of Jairus' daughter to explore it in greater detail. It is recorded in the section of St. Luke's Gospel (8:41-56) that is appointed to be read on the Twenty-fourth Sunday after Pentecost. (See also Matthew 9:18-26 and Mark 5:22-43.)

The Lord had returned from the country of the Gadarenes, where He healed the demon-possessed man, and the people were waiting for Him (Matthew 7:40). It will be remembered that the Gadarenes had asked Him to leave, apparently out of anger at the loss of their swine. St. Ambrose sees in the people of Gadara (also called Gerasa) a figure of the Synagogue, which rejected Christ, and Jesus' departure as a sign of His abandoning the Synagogue. But, in order that not all of His own people might reject Him, "He did not leave the synagogue completely, but reserved a saving remedy for those who might believe in Him" (*Treatise on the Gospel According to St. Luke*, Book 6, no. 54).

"And, behold, there came a man named Jairus, and he was a ruler of the synagogue: and he fell down at Jesus' feet, and besought Him that He would come into his house. For he had one only daughter, about twelve years of age, and she lay a-dying" (8:41-42).

We have pointed out that the young girl's father sought Jesus out. One could conclude that, given St. Ambrose's reference to those Jews "who might believe in Him," Jairus was one who would believe. On the other hand, the Fathers assume that Jairus, as a ruler of the Synagogue, must be one of those who would have put Jesus to death for His miracles. They suspect that despair and the fear of death made him go against his own will and act contrary to his former behavior. (See St. Cyril of Alexandria, *Commentary on the Gospel of St. Luke*, Homily 45.) There is no mention, when Jesus agrees to go to Jairus' house, of the compassion such as He had for the widow of Nain or for Lazarus.

"But as He went the people thronged Him. And a woman having an issue of blood twelve years, which had spent all her living upon physicians, neither could be healed of any, came behind Him, and touched the border of His garment: and immediately her issue of blood stanched" (vv. 42-44).

This woman, the Tradition tells us, spent the rest of her life in the service of Christ and is known as St. Veronica (commemorated on July 12). St. Ambrose, who says that she was a Gentile, finds this significance in her boldness: "While the Word of God is on His way to save the children of Israel in the person of this ruler's daughter, the holy church, which was to be constituted from out of the Gentiles, who were perishing for having fallen into the basest sins, seized by their faith the salvation prepared for others" (*Treatise on the Gospel According to St. Luke*, Book 6, no. 54).

St. John Chrysostom makes no mention of such symbolism. Rather, he stresses the difference between the woman and the ruler of the Synagogue: "Seest thou the woman superior to the ruler of the synagogue? She detained Him not, she took no hold of Him, but touched Him only with the end of her fingers, and though she came later, she first went away healed. And he indeed was bringing the Physician altogether to his house, but for her a mere touch sufficed. For though she was bound by her affliction, yet her faith had given her wings. And mark how He comforts her, saying, 'Thy faith hath saved thee.' Now surely, had He drawn her forward for display, He would not have added this; but He saith this, partly teaching the ruler of the synagogue to believe, partly proclaiming the woman's praise, and affording her by these words delight and advantage equal to her bodily health" (*On the Gospel According to St. Matthew*, Homily 31).

"And Jesus said, Who touched me? When all denied, Peter and they that were with him said, Master the multitude throng thee and press thee, and sayest thou, Who touched me? And Jesus said, Somebody hath touched me: for I perceive that virtue (*dunamin*, "power") is gone out of me" (vv. 45-46).

It seems that Jesus says this in order to draw attention to the woman, who, among all those who thronged Him in turmoil and confusion, was the one person who approached Him in faith. His power responds to that faith, and not to the faithless crowd. (See Blessed Theophylact, *The Explanation of the Holy Gospel According to St. Mark*, ch. 5, vv. 30-34.)

Another contrast between the woman and the ruler is to be found in their perception of His power to heal. She, according to St. Mark, says, "if I may touch but His clothes, I shall be whole" (5:28; see also Matthew 9:21). The ruler, on the other hand, feels that the Lord must be in the presence of his dying daughter and touch her. In St. Matthew's account, the ruler tells Jesus, "My daughter is even now dead, but come and lay thy hand upon her, and she shall live" (9:18). Despite that declaration of confidence, when they reach Jairus' house, they find the usual mourners ("minstrels and the people making a noise"), all of which seems to indicate that those who are of Jairus' household think that it is useless for Jesus to go to her.

With reference to this detail, St. Ambrose says: "It is not without purpose that St. Matthew says that there were in the house minstrels and mourners. For, since they followed the ancient custom, these were brought in so as to inflame and heighten the mourning and crying; in this we see that those of the ruler's household were still of the Synagogue, that is, faithless, and therefore could not capture the joy of the Spirit" (op. cit., no. 64). That is, they saw death as final and had no hope of a resurrection.

We are not told whether the maiden's father and mother were among those who "laughed Him to scorn, knowing that she was dead" (8:53). At any rate, the Lord permits them, along with Peter, James, and John, to accompany Him into the room. On the other hand, He does "put them all out" (8:54) just before restoring her to life and then allows them to see her after the resuscitation. For St. Ambrose (ibid.), the crowd that witnessed the resurrection of the widow's son at Nain represent the response of the Church, composed of many people of all nations that believe on Him, and these witnesses—the three Apostles and two parents—represent those few of the Synagogue who will receive Him as Savior of the world.

When Jesus takes the maiden by the hand and tells her to arise, He immediately orders them to give her food. The widow's son spoke. Jairus' daughter ate. Both actions are signs of life and evidence of their resurrection. After His own resurrection, the Lord demonstrated the reality of His victory over death by the same actions, speaking and eating in the disciples' presence. The raising of the widow's son and the raising of Jairus' daughter are figures of the great and final miracle, Jesus' own resurrection, which gives hope of eternal life to all who put their trust in Him.

13

THE TWENTY-SEVENTH SUNDAY

The Woman with a Spirit of Infirmity (Luke 13:10-17)
The Sabbath-day healing of a woman who was "bowed together" follows the parable of the fruitless fig tree in St. Luke's Gospel (13:10-17). The parable's symbolism, generally accepted by the holy Fathers, has to do with the whole human race but in a special way with the Hebrews. The fig tree

has not produced the fruit that was its nature to produce, and the owner of the vineyard has come every year for three years and found the tree fruitless (13:6-9).

The three years are said to represent the three divisions of time: the first, before the Law was given; the second, after the Law was given; and the third, the time of grace, after the coming of Christ (see St. Augustine, *On the New Testament Lessons*, Homily 60). The dresser of the vineyard represents the righteous of all three periods, the prophets and the saints, who have interceded and intercede for sinful mankind.

The setting for the miracle is a synagogue where the Lord was teaching. Here we find an example of the Lord's visiting His especially chosen people in order to accuse them of failing to bring forth good works and to call them to repentance. The ruler's reaction to the healing of the woman who "had a spirit of infirmity eighteen years" illustrates how radically misunderstood and misused the Law had become among those whom God had so favored and of whom He expected so much.

Some of the Fathers find significance in the number eighteen, the number of years that the woman had suffered. "The perfection of the Law is expressed in the ten words (commandments), while in the number eight the resurrection (to life in the kingdom which is to come) is represented" (St. Ambrose, *Treatise on the Gospel According to St. Luke*, Book 7, no. 173). St. Augustine multiplies the "six" of the days of creation by the "three" of the periods of history to arrive at the number eighteen (ibid.).

The woman's sickness is attributed to the power of Satan. The Gospel speaks of "a spirit of infirmity," and the Savior Himself regards her as one "whom Satan hath bound."

"The woman, therefore, who was bowed together is said to have suffered from the cruelty of the devil...; God, as I have said, so permitting it, either for her own sins, or rather by the operation of a universal and general law" (St. Cyril of Alexandria, *Commentary on the Gospel of St. Luke*, Homily 96). The Lord heals her first by His word—"Woman, thou art loosed from thine infirmity"—and then by His touch: "He laid His hands on her: and immediately she was made straight, and glorified God" (vv. 12-13).

This miracle is remarkable for two reasons: first, neither was the woman seeking to be healed, nor did anyone else intercede for her; second, the Lord demonstrates that He is the incarnate God by the simple declaration that she was loosed. His power over Satan as God and man is manifested from the beginning, at His temptation immediately after His baptism and in all His miracles (see St. Athanasius, *Against the Arians*, Discourse 3).

The ruler of the synagogue, for whom religion consisted of the observance of laws that could not be set aside even for mercy's sake, condemned the Lord for healing on the Sabbath. God's rest from His works on the seventh day was commemorated by the Hebrews on the Sabbath, and it is the rest to which all the godly and righteous believers in Christ are called (see Hebrews 4). Just as God's providence never ceases to operate, never rests, so also Christ does not rest from doing good on the Sabbath. As He says on another occasion when the Jews object to His healing on the Sabbath: "My Father worketh hitherto, and I work" (John 5:17).

Of course, the Lord convicts them as ignorant of the very thing in which they should be better instructed than anyone. "Thou hypocrite, doth not each one of you on the Sabbath loose his ox or his ass from the stall, and lead him away to watering? And ought not this woman, being a daughter of Abraham, whom Satan hath bound, lo, these eighteen years, be loosed from this bond on the Sabbath day?" (vv. 15-16).

The rejection of Christ as the incarnate God by the Jews is matched by the heretics who claim that the eternal God could not possibly humble Himself and condescend to take on our nature. The heretic reasons that Christ must be a created being. "Do you conceive of Him as less...because He humbles Himself for the sake of the soul that is bent down to the ground, that He may exalt with Himself that which is bent double under the weight of sin?" (St. Gregory of Nazianzus, *Second Oration on Pascha*, 36).

So, as we see on other occasions, His enemies, the reputed guardians of religion, "were ashamed: and all the people rejoiced for all the glorious things that were done by Him" (Luke 13:17).

14

THE TWENTY-NINTH SUNDAY

The Ten Lepers (Luke 17:12-19)

The healing of lepers recorded in Luke 17:12-19 is not the first such healing. Earlier in the same Gospel (5:12-13), we find Jesus healing one man so afflicted in response to his cry: "Lord, if thou wilt, thou canst make me clean." We read in the present miracle of ten men "that were lepers, which stood afar off: and they lifted up their voices, and said, Jesus, Master, have mercy on us" (17:12-13).

There are two important differences to be noted in these narratives. Note, first, the complete confidence in Christ's power expressed by the single leper: "if thou wilt, thou canst..." In the other case, although there is obviously some degree of trust, the ten make a plea simply for "mercy." Secondly, the Lord actually touches the man in Chapter 5 and pronounces the cleansing: "I will. Be thou clean." In the present case, the ten find healing as they go in obedience to His command. That is, the Lord heals them from a distance.

In both cases, the Lord orders them "to go shew" themselves "unto the priests" (5:14; 17:14). Why does He do this?

"It was because the Jews, using ever as a pretext their respect for the Law, and saying that Moses the 'hierophant' (interpreter of sacred mysteries) was the minister of a commandment from on high, made it their endeavor to treat with contempt Christ the Savior of us all. They even said plainly: 'We know that God spake unto Moses, but this man, we know not whence He is'" (John 9:29) (St. Cyril of Alexandria, *Commentary on the Gospel of St. Luke*, Homily on ch. 5). Practically, too, it was necessary, given the respect for the Law prevalent in that society, that there be a testimony to the fact that they were clean indeed. Only the priests could give it.

The Venerable Bede cites yet another reason: "We find that none of those to whom the Lord gave bodily favors were sent to the priests save the lepers. For the priesthood of the Jews was a figure of the Royal Priesthood to come, which is the Church, and in which all are consecrated who belong to the Body of Christ, the True and Supreme High Priest" (*Exposition of the Gospel*, cited by M. F. Toal, *The Sunday Sermons of the Great Fathers*, Vol. IV, p. 84).

In neither case does the Lord indicate that He wants to reveal Himself for who He is by means of this type of healing. In fact, in the first, He specifically "charged him to tell no man" (v. 14), although the leprosy left him immediately. The emphasis in Luke 17 is quite different. It would seem very normal for anyone, on discovering that he had been cleansed, to turn back to acknowledge the Healer, give thanks, and to tell what had happened. Only one "returned to give glory to God" (v. 18).

That one "was a Samaritan" (v. 16). The others, apparently Jews, were so concerned about the testimony of the priests that they never thought to give thanks. This, of course, is not the only time the Lord shows the Samaritans to be more responsive to the higher laws of mercy and thanksgiving and receptive to Him. Consider the Parable of the Good Samaritan

(Luke 10:25-37) and the meeting with the Samaritan woman at the well (John 4).

Leprosy, a dread and highly infectious disease, is encountered frequently in the Old Testament. It was perhaps the most feared of diseases. Leviticus 13 and 14 offer elaborate prescriptions for the cleansing, or testifying to the cleansing, of a leper. The disease was feared not only because of the disastrous physical manifestations but also because it was generally thought to be a penalty for grievous sins. Lepers were more often the object of contempt and derision than of pity. They were shut off from society. The ten "stood afar off" because of the shame which, justly or unjustly, they were made to feel.

The Old Testament priest could not heal the disease; he could only observe and testify as to whether the contamination had spread or whether there had been a spontaneous remission. He could declare a leper "unclean" or "cleansed." The Lord's ability to heal this most dreaded affliction, far from drawing the priests' admiration, fills them with jealousy and anger. And since He healed both physically and spiritually, His enemies seized upon His forgiving sins to accuse Him of blasphemy. If He healed on the Sabbath, He was accused of violating the Law.

The lessons for us are several. We ought always to be grateful to God for all we receive, giving thanks and glorifying God in prayer. Even when we get what we pray for, we often take the benefit for granted and forget to give thanks. Also, we must never judge another, find fault with the good things another does, just because he does not have the right faith, or any faith at all. In our pride, we often find it hard to believe that God would favor a heretic or a pagan. Are we foolish enough to think we can limit God's mercy? Finally, we must be attentive to our own ills, especially the spiritual ones. Pride often makes us think that something that is reprehensible in another person is a trifle in ourselves. Let us also understand that we may be "spiritual lepers," in deep need of God's healing mercy.

15

THE THIRTY-FIRST SUNDAY

The Blind Man (Luke 18:35-43)

The restoration of sight to a blind man is recorded in each of the synoptic Gospels: Matthew 20:29-34; Mark 10:46-52; and Luke 18:35-43. St. Luke's account is the reading for the Thirty-first Sunday after Pentecost.

This incident takes place while the Lord and those who follow Him are going up to Jerusalem, after He has told them what must happen there. "Behold, we go up to Jerusalem, and all things that are written by the prophets concerning the Son of man shall be accomplished" (Luke 18:31; Matthew 20:18-19; Mark 10:33-34). In Matthew and Mark, between the Lord's prophecy of His passion and the present miracle, we find James and John asking to sit one on the Lord's right hand and the other on His left in His kingdom. (In Matthew their mother makes the request.)

Differences in detail that would make the three narratives contradict one another are not to be found. There are explanations of them in the writings of the Fathers, including St. John Chrysostom, St. Augustine, and St. Ambrose. Some say simply that we have the record as the Evangelists remembered them; but most say that, although all three writers are equally inspired by the Holy Spirit, they had the freedom to give emphasis to different features of the incident. St. Matthew speaks of two blind men; St. Mark and St. Luke mention but one. The consensus is that there were probably two, one of them well-known or simply the spokesman for both. That he was at least known is demonstrated by St. Mark's identifying him by name, Bartimaeus, the son of Timaeus. Both St. Mark and St. Luke describe him as sitting by the wayside and begging (see St. Augustine, *The Harmony of the Gospels*, ch. 65).

"And it came to pass, that as He was nigh unto Jericho, a certain blind man sat by the way side begging: and hearing the multitude pass by, he asked what it meant. And they told him, that Jesus of Nazareth passeth by. And he cried, saying, Jesus, thou Son of David, have mercy of me" (vv. 35-38).

The blind man must ask, of course, what went on about him. The answer, that Jesus of Nazareth was passing by, was in accordance with what the crowd saw and understood; this Jesus was a man whom many considered to be a prophet. The blind man, on the other hand, was able to know who Jesus really was, and he called Him "Son of David...Lord." "Who has taught you to speak thus, O man? Have you, though deprived of sight, read Scriptures? How have you discerned the Light of the world? Truly, 'the Lord enlighteneth the blind' (Psalm 145:8)" (St. Cyril of Alexandria, *Homily on the Gospel*). "There was a multitude of people around the person of Jesus: the blind man could not see the Light of Truth, but in his soul he could feel His presence...He is told one thing, and cries another...They who could see made answer from what was known by common report, but the blind man made known what he had learned from the Truth Itself" (from a homily attributed to St. John Chrysostom).

"And they which went before rebuked him, that he should hold his peace: but he cried so much the more, Thou Son of David, have mercy on me" (v. 39).

Exactly who "they" were is not clear, but they must have regarded the title he gave Jesus, as well as his petition, as inappropriate. It is likely that they rejected the title, since it was one normally given to the expected Messiah. Even if they had great respect for this "prophet," they were not ready to admit that

kind of confession. It is not likely that they were just concerned citizens who wanted to see good order maintained, or
that they did not want Jesus to be interrupted as He went along
teaching. In any event, the Fathers are practically unanimous
in seeing this rebuke or reprimand as a figure of the forces that
strive to keep one from confessing Christ. St. Gregory the
Great says: "Whom do they signify, who went before Jesus, as
He came, if not the crowd of carnal desires, and the tumult of
the vices, which, before Christ makes entry into our hearts,
scatter our thoughts with their temptations and confuse the
pleading of the soul in prayer...For often when we desire to
turn again to the Lord...the images of the sins we have committed rise against us, they war against the fervor of our soul, they
darken the spirit, and strive to silence the voice of our suppli-
cation" (*Homily on the Gospel*). St. Augustine makes another
application: "The crowd clamors, that the blind man shall not
cry out. There are not a few Christians who seek to hinder us
from living as Christians: like the crowd that walked with
Christ, and hindered the man crying out to Christ and hungering
for light from the kindness of Christ. There are such Christians:
but let us overcome them, and live in virtue: and our life shall
be the voice of our cry to Christ...They who shall persevere in
doing such things as Christ has enjoined, and regard not the
multitudes that hinder them...but who love the light which
Christ is about to restore to them, more than they fear the uproar
of those who are hindering them, they shall in no wise be separated from Him" (*Sermons on the Gospel Lessons*).

II

1

THE FIRST SIGN: THE WEDDING AT CANA
(John 2:1-11)

We have completed our discussion of the miracles of Christ that are recorded in the Gospel readings for the Thirty-two Sundays after Pentecost. The next section will deal with the miracles (or "signs") that are found in the Holy Gospel of St. John. We will study them in order.

The section of St. John's Gospel that contains the brief story of the marriage feast in Cana of Galilee is appointed to be read during weddings in our Church. The prayers of the rite make reference to the Lord's presence as the source of blessing for all marriages and as the reason that matrimony is considered one of the holy mysteries or sacraments. But the texts of the prayers do not draw attention to any of the details that are mentioned in the eleven verses of the section.

The same section is read on another occasion, the Monday after Thomas Sunday. During the Paschal season, St. John is read, with few exceptions, on all days: weekdays, Saturdays, and Sundays. Since the early days of the Church, this season has been a period of instruction for new Christians who were baptized and chrismated at Pascha. They had already received the fundamental teachings of the Faith. Now they were in the proper state to have their initiation explained. They had been baptized and chrismated; they had received communion. What did it all mean? That is the question that the post-baptismal instruction addressed, and its basis was St. John's Gospel. Why St. John? Because it was recognized that the Lord's miracles are really "signs" (*semeion* is the Greek word that St. John uses) pointing to the sacramental basis of the Christian life.

There are signs, for example, in which water is not only a necessary element for cleansing or for satisfying the thirst, but also symbolic of the water of baptism.

It is evident throughout the New Testament that Christ's presence transforms everything. The signs bear witness to that transformation. This is especially true in the fourth Gospel. St. John's use of certain elements—water, bread, wine—and their continued use in the holy mysteries are a sign of the Lord's presence.

The story of the wedding feast is told in few words, but each seems to say something more than it normally does. This has led some commentators to conclude that the marriage feast is more a parable than a real event. Generally, the Fathers of the Church treat it as a real happening but one full of significance.

"And the third day there was a marriage in Cana of Galilee, and the mother of Jesus was there" (John 2:1).

Why does St. John mention "the third day?" Do the days referred to in the foregoing verses of the first chapter plus this one present a simple sequence of events on three successive days? It is not perfectly clear from the record that begins with 1:19 where to start numbering the days. Actually, there appear to be five days on which something significant happens. Still, the Evangelist has called the day of the wedding "the third day," and it is, chronologically, if we take verse 29 as our starting point, but even here, the verse begins with "the next day." Some think that the meaning is quite simple, since Wednesday, the third day of the week, was a day for weddings, according to the Talmud. On the other hand, in light of the rich symbolism of the rest of the story, we must conclude that the third day has some connection with the Lord's rising from the dead on the third day, when His hour and His glorification had already come.

If we follow the sequence of events in the first chapter of the Gospel, after the prologue, first we find the Pharisees questioning John the Baptist about who he is and why he is baptizing. He calls himself "the voice of one crying in the wilderness, Make straight the way of the Lord" (v. 23). He is the Lord's prophet and forerunner: "After me cometh a man which is preferred before me: for He was before me" (v. 30). The man upon whom he saw the Spirit descending "is the Son of God" (v. 34).

Now on the first "next day" John recognizes Jesus as the one about whom he had prophesied: "Behold the Lamb of God, which taketh away the sin of the world" (v. 29). And on the second "next day" two of John's disciples, on hearing his declaration, leave him to follow Jesus (v. 37). One is Andrew, who then proclaims to his own brother, Simon (Peter), that "We have found the Messiah" (v. 41). Then, on "the day following," Jesus finds His third disciple, Philip, who in turn finds Nathanael and brings him to Jesus. Nathanael confesses that Jesus is the Son of God, the King of Israel (v. 49).

So on these days we see the end of Old Testament prophecy in John's recognition of Jesus as the One whom he had foretold. In addition, his own ministry gives way to that of Jesus, as we see two of John's disciples leave him to follow Jesus. Further, we see the calling of the first disciples, the beginning of the Church.

Now, the marriage on the third day has the blessing of the Son of God, His very presence. But it also provides the occasion for His first sign, the changing of the water into wine. Let us again call attention to the fact that the miracles of our Lord are never self-contained; that is, they were not performed just to demonstrate His power, except when He felt it necessary to show that He had power to forgive sins. That the miracles point to something greater and of deeper significance than the acts themselves becomes evident in the brief conversation between Jesus and His mother. She had interceded for the host and the guests: "They have no wine." Jesus' reply seems at first to be a refusal: "Woman, what have I to do with thee? mine hour is not yet come."

This first part of this answer, as it is translated, has given rise to the opinion that the Lord is informing His mother, even disrespectfully, that He has nothing to do with her and more or less separates Himself from her and her intervention. The Greek original literally means, "What is it to me and to thee?" In view of the second part of the reply, "mine hour is not yet come," which gives the key to the whole incident, we have to conclude that the literal translation is the more appropriate one. In any case, we could understand that He is saying either, "this is not our business" or "I have nothing to do with thee at this particular moment or for this purpose."

Jesus' "hour" cannot be understood as the moment when He was to begin to perform miracles. The references to His hour and its meaning are proof of this. In St. John's Gospel, we find: "The Jews sought to take Him, and no man laid his hand on Him, because His hour was not yet come" (7:30). "These words spake He as He taught in the temple: and no man took Him: because His hour was not yet come" (8:20). "My time (*kairos*) is not yet come" (7:6). "Jesus answereth them saying: the hour is come that the Son of Man should be glorified" (12:23). And this clear reference to His death: "Now before the feast of the Passover, Jesus knowing that His hour was come that He should depart out of this world unto the Father" (13:1). Finally, in His prayer to the Father just before His death: "Father, the hour is come. Glorify thy Son" (17:1). There can be no doubt that all of these expressions refer to the time of His death, His redeeming sacrifice.

In view of the fact that the Lord's "hour was not yet come," and that He proceeds, nevertheless, to do the very thing that His mother has asked Him to do, we have to conclude that the miracle of changing water into wine is a sign of a greater future miracle. In spite of what at first appears to be a refusal, she obviously does not understand it that way. Her next words to the servants, "Whatever He saith unto you, do it," indicate that she knew He would comply with her request.

One further comment on Jesus' reply to His mother: the reasons for His addressing her as "Woman" have been deduced in widely differing ways. Some Bible readers, refusing to acknowledge any role of the Virgin in the story of redemption, see this designation as proof of the Lord's rejecting her and of His declaring His independence from her. We must reject that approach outright. The Lord's mother would not have understood Him in this way, as we see from what she did immediately afterward.

"Woman" was not the usual way for a son to address his mother. On the Lord's lips it must have some significance. In order to understand His meaning, we must recall that He addresses her the same way on another occasion. From the cross He says, "Woman, behold thy son." At the time when His "hour had indeed come," that of His glorification, His death on the cross, to be followed by His resurrection, the ultimate miracle, if you will, He calls her "Woman." "When Jesus therefore saw His mother, and the disciple standing by, whom He loved, He saith unto His mother, Woman, behold thy son! Then saith He to the disciple, Behold thy mother! And from that hour that disciple took her into his own home" (John 19:26, 27). (The explanation offered by some that Jesus was merely providing His mother with a home is weak. Too many relations and in-laws were around for her to be left homeless.) The resurrection brings victory over death and over that of which death is the "wages," sin. One cannot help but recall that the first promise of the redemption, at the beginning of its history, was made concerning the first woman, Eve: "her (the

woman's) seed (descendant) shall bruise thy head (the ser-
pent's/the devil's)." Mary is the new Eve, in Orthodox Tradition, the one who, unlike the first, heard the word of God and
kept it, the one who was perfectly obedient to the will of God.
The designation "Woman" thus has profound significance. It
has nothing of the disrespect that a superficial consideration of
the passage might suggest. Eve, the mother of all living (Genesis 3), that is, of all the human race, is now replaced by the new
Eve, and here precisely she becomes the mother of all those
who have been born again into the life in Christ, who are represented by the beloved disciple John.

St. Luke records things concerning the Virgin's participa-
tion in the Lord's life and work that the other Gospel writers do
not. He writes of her reaction to the shepherds' report concerning what they had heard from the angels about the newborn
child, and of her reaction to Jesus' own words when, at the age
of twelve, He had stayed behind in Jerusalem, to the puzzle-
ment of both the mother and the foster-father. In both cases, it
is recorded that she kept these things in her heart (2:19, 51).
Further, at Jesus' presentation in the temple, Simeon the righteous Elder, recognizing who this Child was, said specifically
to Mary His mother (not to the two "parents"): "Behold, this
child is set for the fall and rising of many in Israel; and for a
sign which shall be spoken against; yea, a sword shall pierce
through thine own soul also, that the thoughts of many hearts
may be revealed" (2:34-35). Thus, not only did she remember
the things that had been said about Him and by Him, but she
had a prophecy from the righteous Simeon that directly concerned her. In other words, she was conscious of who He was,
for the Angel had told her that He would be called the Son of
God (1:35), and she had also been given some knowledge of
His mission. Thus again, in spite of the paucity of specific
mentions, it is evident from the crucial points in His life where

she is mentioned that she accompanied Him both physically and spiritually all His life, from birth to death.

We have drawn attention to the economy of words and details in the narrative of Christ's presence at the marriage feast in Cana. But we have also insisted that each word and each detail is both carefully chosen and filled with significance. There is no doubt that the story refers to a real incident, but it is reported here in the fourth Gospel a few years or many years after the other Gospels were written. It is likely that theological reflection and experience, principally liturgical experience, made it possible for the writer to explore and explain the deeper significance of the events of the life of our Lord.

When we say "liturgical experience," we make special reference to baptism and the eucharist, since it is quite clear from the Acts of the Apostles and the epistles that these mysteries were the pre-eminent elements in the life of the early Church. The signs and their interpretation, reported in St. John's Gospel, reveal the transforming effect of Christ's presence and then imply that that same transforming presence will be at work in the holy mysteries. The interpretation is generally provided by an alteration in terminology or the addition of details not found in parallel accounts, when they exist, in the three synoptic Gospels.

Most of the signs center on water, bread, or wine, the very matter of the two holy mysteries we have mentioned. Jesus reveals His messiahship to the Samaritan woman, speaking to her of living water (ch. 4). He heals the paralytic at the pool of Bethesda (ch. 5). He feeds the five thousand miraculously (ch. 6). He restores the sight of a blind man, sending him to wash in the pool of Siloam (ch. 9). The two sections that unmistakably describe the effects of baptism and the eucharist are found in Chapters 3 and 6. In the conversation with Nicodemus, the Lord declares that "except a man be born again...of water and the Spirit, he cannot enter into the kingdom of God" (3:3, 5). After feeding the five thousand, the Lord says, "Except ye eat the flesh of the Son of man, and drink His blood, ye have no life in you" (6:53). St. Paul, explaining how believers eat the flesh and drink the blood of Christ, warns the Corinthians that "whosoever shall eat of this bread and drink of this cup of the Lord, unworthily, shall be guilty of the body and blood of the Lord" (1 Corinthians 11:27). The same Apostle explains the rebirth in his epistle to the Romans: "Therefore we are buried with Him into death (in baptism): that like as Christ was raised up from the dead by the glory of the Father, even so we also should walk in newness of life" (6:4).

There is no doubt that St. John uses certain terms and details in the story of the first miracle to emphasize its sacramental and worship significance. The servants whom Jesus directs to fill the waterpots are not called by the usual word for servants: they are called *diakonoi* (deacons). That designation no doubt derives from the experience of deacons as servants of the mysteries; it also enhances the worship atmosphere of the incident.

The waterpots were special pots, "after the manner of the purifying of the Jews." The guests had participated, according to custom, in the ritual purification to enter "worthily" into the marriage ceremony and the feast. The water cleansing of the Jews was symbolic of the real and effective purification offered by the Savior. The new wine, apparently an enormous quantity of it (some 120 gallons or more), contrasts sharply with the old wine. The joy of the people at an earthly marriage, for which they were prepared by their washing and had entered into somewhat inadequately by their partaking of the first wine, becomes a much greater joy when this new wine, divinely provided, becomes available at the end (the good wine when all have drunk sufficiently). Thus will those who follow

Christ, born again in the washing of baptism, and nourished by the saving blood of Christ in the eucharist, experience the complete joy of the kingdom.

It is significant that the scene of this first sign is a wedding and that the One who will call Himself the Bridegroom is present (Mark 2:19-20). He is the Bridegroom of the parable of the ten virgins (Matthew 25:1-13). He is also called the Bridegroom by St. John (3:29). In Ephesians (5:22-32), St. Paul explains the relationship of Christ to His Church as that of the Bridegroom with His bride (see also 2 Corinthians 11:2). Israel, destined to become the bride of God, had failed and been unfaithful (see Isaiah 54:5 and Psalm 45). The true Bridegroom, of whom all earthly bridegrooms are a figure, has come to claim His true bride, all those who truly believe in Him and have entered by being born of water and the Spirit into His kingdom and are nourished at His banquet table.

2

THE SECOND SIGN: THE NOBLEMAN'S SON (John 4:46-54)

The second miracle (or sign) that Jesus did after He came out of Judea and into Galilee is recorded in St. John 4:46-54. This sign, the healing of a nobleman's son, follows the Lord's extraordinary conversation with the Samaritan woman at Jacob's well (vv. 1-42) and His acceptance by the Samaritans. The people of that city urge Him to stay, and he does, for two days (v. 40).

"So Jesus came again into Cana of Galilee, where He made the water wine" (v. 46). Why does the Evangelist call our attention to the Lord's first sign? St. John Chrysostom says that it is "to remind the hearer to exalt the praise of the Samaritans" (*On the Gospel According to St. John*, Homily 35). As will be made clear, the inhabitants of Jesus' own land, Galilee, believed in Him because of His miracles; the Samaritans believed because of His teaching. "And many more (Samaritans) believed because of His own word...Then when He was come into Galilee, the Galileans received Him, having seen all the things that He did at Jerusalem, for they also went unto the feast" (vv. 41, 45). Jesus even says to the nobleman interceding for his son, "Except ye see signs and wonders, ye will not believe" (v. 48).

The Evangelist reports that Jesus went into Galilee, the implication being, *Galilee rather than Jerusalem*. A saying of Jesus recorded in the synoptic Gospels is repeated here: "A prophet hath no honour in his own country" (see Matthew 13:57, Mark 6:4, and Luke 4:24). While the synoptic Evangelists use "his own country" to refer to the land where Jesus was brought up, to Nazareth, it is evident throughout St. John's Gospel that Jerusalem, the heart of the Jewish nation, is, in a spiritual sense, the Lord's earthly country, His own land.

The Fourth Gospel's recollection of the first sign, the changing of the water into wine at Cana, seems to establish a link to the present sign, the healing of the nobleman's son. Beneath this exercise of Jesus' mighty power lies another theme of general application: the relation of faith to life—life eternal.

Why had Jesus gone to Cana? St. John Chrysostom raises that question and offers an answer: "At first He came, being invited to a marriage; but why now? It seems to me, to confirm by His presence the faith that had been implanted by His miracle (sign), and to draw them to Him all the more by coming to them self-invited, by leaving His own country and by preferring them" (ibid.).

"And there was a certain nobleman, whose son was sick at Capernaum. When he heard that Jesus was come out of Judea into Galilee, he went unto Him, and besought Him that He would come down, and heal his son: for he was at the point of death" (vv. 46-47).

Some commentators, including very ancient ones, have attempted to identify the nobleman. Some have said that he is the centurion who, in St. Matthew's Gospel (8:5), comes to Jesus at Capernaum and asks Him to heal his "servant." Commentators who take this view note that both the centurion and the father use the same Greek word, *pais*, which can mean either "child" or "servant." However, St. John uses a more specific word, *huios*, "son," in v. 46; furthermore, the Lord Himself uses the same term when He assures the nobleman that "thy *son* liveth" (v. 50). Other commentators are convinced that because the man is called *vasilikos*, "courtier" or "royal official," he must have been in the service of Herod Antipas, the tetrarch of Galilee and Persia from 4 B.C. to A.D. 39. That may very well be true, but the question remains, Was this *vasilikos* a centurion? We cannot know for sure, but, ultimately, this has little to do with the sign and the reason for its placement in the Fourth Gospel.

The following is St. John Chrysostom's opinion in this regard: "This person certainly was of royal race, or possessed some dignity from his office, to which the title 'noble' was attached. Some indeed think that this is the man mentioned by Matthew (8:5), but he is shown to be a different person, not only from his dignity, but also from his faith. That other, even when Christ was willing to go with him, entreats Him to tarry; this one, when He had made no such offer, draws Him to his house. The one saith, 'I am not worthy that Thou shouldest come under my roof'; but this other even urges Him, saying, 'Come down ere my son die.' In that instance He came down from the mountain, and entered into Capernaum; but here, as He came from Samaria, and went not into Capernaum but into Cana, this person met Him. The servant of the other was possessed by the palsy, this one's son by a fever" (ibid.).

Concerning the nobleman and his faith, St. John Chrysostom goes on to say: "Yet the very coming and beseeching Him was a mark of faith. And besides, after this the Evangelist witnesses to him, declaring that when Jesus said, 'Go, thy son liveth,' he believed, and went...And so if this ruler also believed, yet he believed not entirely or soundly, as is clear from his inquiring 'at what hour the fever left him,' since he desired to know whether it did so of its own accord, or at the bidding of Christ. When therefore he knew that it was 'yesterday at the seventh hour,' then 'himself believed and his whole house' " (*On the Gospel According to St. John*, Homily 35).

Jesus chides the nobleman (and the people of Capernaum) with those words, "Except ye see signs and wonders, ye will not believe," in order to "touch his conscience, to show that His miracles were wrought principally for the sake of the soul. For here He heals the father, sick in mind, no less than the son, in order to persuade us to give heed to Him, not by reason of His miracles, but of His teaching. For miracles are not for the faithful, but for the unbelieving" (ibid.).

The healing of the "certain nobleman's son" demonstrates the Lord's healing power, of course, but its significance is greater by far. Its primary importance lies in its relation to two themes we find in the second, third and fourth chapters of this Gospel: the content of the Good News and its universality.

The marriage feast at Cana, the Lord's conversation with Nicodemus, the remarkable encounter with the Samaritan woman, the healing of the nobleman's son—the Evangelist uses these incidents to show the Lord not only fulfilling His purpose in coming to His chosen people but also going beyond them to announce the Good News to the whole world. At the heart of this Good News is the gift that He brings to all peoples, the gift of eternal life.

Note the progression of His encounters: The Lord interacts with a Jew (Nicodemus), a Samaritan (the woman at the well), and a Gentile (the nobleman). We find the same pattern for the spread of the Gospel in the Lord's last words to His disciples just before the Ascension: "Ye shall receive power, after that the Holy Spirit is come upon you: and ye shall be witnesses unto me both in Jerusalem, and in all Judea, and in Samaria, and unto the uttermost parts of the earth" (Acts 1:8).

In His dealings with Nicodemus and the Samaritan woman, the Lord reveals certain essential theological truths, and the theme is unmistakably eternal or everlasting life (John 3:15, 16; 4:14, etc.). And during His encounter with the Gentile nobleman, He gives life to a dying person as a token of His ultimate purpose, the gift of life to the world.

The reason for the Evangelist's reference to the first sign (4:46, 54) becomes clear: By changing water into wine—and not just any water, but specifically the water of Jewish purification rites—the Lord symbolically demonstrates that the rites of purification are being replaced by the all-sufficient purification offered to mankind in the blood of His own sacrifice. Later He will say that "except ye eat the flesh of the Son of man and drink His blood, ye have no life in you" (6:53). Later still, He will declare the wine of the Last Supper to be His blood: "Drink ye all of it" (Matthew 26:27).

The Good News—the message of reconciliation and redemption through Christ's life, His passion, crucifixion, burial and resurrection—is the constant theme of the Fourth Gospel. Figures of the holy mysteries (sacraments) abound, particularly baptism and the eucharist, and their relation to these saving acts is made clear. It is in them that the continuing presence of Christ transforms those who partake of them. The mysteries become the means for all people of all times to participate in the effects of those saving acts.

From the Lord's conversation with Nicodemus, we learn that "except a man be born again (from on high), he cannot see the kingdom of God" (3:3). Further, as the Lord explains, "Except a man be born of water and of the Spirit, he cannot enter into the kingdom of God" (v. 5). This water rebirth is obviously baptism. St. Paul later takes up the theme and explains exactly what are the effects of this holy mystery: "Know ye not, that so many of us as were baptized into Jesus Christ, were baptized into His death? ...If we are dead with Christ, we believe that we shall also live with Him" (Romans 6:3, 8).

3

THE THIRD SIGN: THE PARALYTIC
(John 5:1-15)

The healing of the paralytic at the Sheep's Pool is the third "sign" recorded in St. John's Gospel (5:1-15). Although the Evangelist does not refer to it as the third, nor does he expressly link it to the two previous signs, he does develop a theme implied in his account of the healing of the nobleman's son: Jesus' relation to the people of His own country or land.

The remainder of Chapter 5 contains Jesus' exposition of His own identity, His relation to John the Baptist, and, more importantly, to His heavenly Father. The miracle provides the impetus for the theological revelations to follow, and so we need to get a grasp on the chapter as a whole. It may be outlined as follows:

1. The miracle and its symbolism.

2. The question of the meaning of the Sabbath.

3. The Lord's exposition of His relation to the Father.

4. The role of St. John the Baptist.

5. The failure of the Jews.

This is not the only instance of a healing on the Sabbath, and it is useful to review other such cases. We have treated one of them in an earlier chapter on the reading for the Twenty-seventh Sunday after Pentecost (Luke 13:10-17).

In every other case—in Matthew, Mark, and Luke—the Lord briefly answers the objections of the Jews and Pharisees, usually making one essential point. Whether He expanded the point on those occasions we cannot know.

So as not to omit a particularly important declaration by the Lord, we will begin with the incident from St. Luke. Our Lord healed a woman who had had "a spirit of infirmity" for eighteen years, and His good work met with the accustomed opposition, but He put His adversaries to shame. His answer showed His deep compassion, but He made no declaration concerning Himself. "Doth not each one of you on the Sabbath loose his ox or his ass from the stall, and lead him away to watering? And ought not this woman, being a daughter of Abraham, whom Satan hath bound, lo, these eighteen years, be loosed from this bond on the Sabbath day?" (vv. 15-16).

In the next chapter, the Lord sets the stage for the healing of the man with the dropsy by asking the lawyers and Pharisees whether it is lawful to heal on the Sabbath. Here, both before the healing and after His question, which is similar to the one in the preceding incident, they remain silent (See Luke 14:1-6).

In St. Mark's Gospel (2:23-28), when the Pharisees criticize the disciples for plucking ears of corn on the Sabbath, He reminds them how David once asked for and ate the shewbread in the house of God and gave it to those who were with him, a story found in 1 Samuel (1 Kings) 21:1-6. Jesus declares, "The Sabbath was made for man, and not man for the Sabbath." And further, "The Son of man is Lord also of the Sabbath."

St. Matthew reports the same incident. Again, Jesus recalls the David story. He recalls, too, how the priests had violated the day of rest (see Numbers 28:9-10). But He also makes a veiled allusion to the fact that He will replace the temple as the place of God's presence: "In this place is one greater than the temple" (12:6).

In the synoptic accounts, Jesus convincingly justifies violating the Sabbath law, but we do not find in them the sort of elaborate theological exposition that St. John records. We might conclude that it fell especially to the Fourth Evangelist to report the Lord's rather detailed theological declarations to complete what the other three did not see fit to include.

The narrative in John 5 begins thus: "After this there was a feast of the Jews; and Jesus went up to Jerusalem. Now there is at Jerusalem by the sheep market a pool, which is called in the Hebrew tongue Bethesda, having five porches." Commentators are divided as to which feast is referred to. St. John Chrysostom favors Pentecost (*On the Gospel According to St. John*, Homily 36). The Evangelist does not tell us, and we may assume that the specifics have no particular bearing on the incident. Other details, and St. John's love of symbolism, lead us to believe that he was sure that the Lord had chosen this place and the paralytic for their symbolic value. St. Augustine says that the "five porches in which the infirm folk lay signify the Law, which was first given to the Jews and to the people of Israel by Moses the servant of God. For this Moses the minister of the Law wrote five books...The five porches figured the Law" (*Sermons on New Testament Lessons*, Sermon 75, no. 2).

St. John's account of the healing of the paralytic is read on the Fourth Sunday of Pascha. On the Wednesday following, the Feast of Mid-Pentecost is celebrated.

The Feast of Feasts—the Resurrection of our Lord, God, and Savior Jesus Christ from the dead—was from the beginning of the Church's work in the world the most appropriate occasion for baptizing catechumens after their long period of instruction. This is so because, in the words of St. Paul, "we are buried with Him in baptism, wherein also ye are risen with Him through the faith of the operation of God, who hath raised Him from the dead" (Colossians 2:12; see Romans 6:4). St. Peter also testifies to this conviction of the Church, recalling how eight souls in Noah's ark were "saved through water": "The like figure whereunto baptism doth also now save us (not the putting away of the filth of the flesh, but the answer of a good conscience toward God), by the resurrection of Jesus Christ" (1 Peter 3:20-21).

At the commemoration of the Lord's triumph over death, each person's own victory over death in his baptism is celebrated. Baptism is the means whereby one becomes a participant in the death, burial, and resurrection of Christ.

The baptismal character of the Paschal feast is evident especially when, at the Liturgy, the Trisagion is replaced by the biblical hymn, "As many as have been baptized into Christ have put on Christ, Alleluia" (Galatians 3:27).

The 40 days after Pascha are a time, just as in the early Church, when Christians rejoice in their Lord's and their own victory over death. It is a time for those who have been incorporated by baptism into Christ's mystical Body, the Church, to receive further instruction in the holy mysteries, especially baptism and the holy eucharist, of which they have only recently become partakers. The *Catechetical Lectures* of St. Cyril of Jerusalem give clear evidence of the continuation of this practice in his times. He tells the newly illuminated that, now having experienced these things, they are in the proper condition to understand his teaching of "the deep meaning for them of what was done on that evening of their baptism" (*Mystagogical Catechesis*, 1, 1).

The lessons for the paschal season reflect this concern that both the newly received and the long-standing faithful understand the holy mysteries. The readings are taken almost exclusively from the Gospel of St. John, for he, as is well-known, establishes a relationship between the Lord's signs and teachings and these two great mysteries.

That there is a deep relationship between the lesson for the Fourth Sunday of Pascha and the mystery of holy baptism is evident in some of the hymns and verses from the Pentecostarion, the Church's service book for this season:

"Of old an Angel came down to the Sheep's Pool and healed one man every year, but now Christ doth cleanse endless multitudes by divine Baptism" ("Matins for the Sunday of the Paralytic," Canon, Ode 1; also Ode 4).

St. John Chrysostom writes: "What manner of cure is this? What mystery doth it signify to us? For these things are not written carelessly, or without a purpose, but as by a figure and type they show in outline things to come, in order that what was exceedingly strange might not by coming unexpectedly harm the faith of the hearers. What then is it that they show in outline? A Baptism was about to be given, possessing much power, and the greatest of gifts, a Baptism purging all sins, and making men alive instead of dead. These things then are foreshown as in a picture by the pool, and by many other circumstances. And first is given a water which purges the stains of our bodies, and those defilements which are not, but seem to be, as those from touching the dead, those from leprosy, and other similar causes; under the old covenant one may see many things done by water on this account...Around this pool 'lay a great multitude of impotent folk, of blind, halt, withered, waiting for the moving of the water; but then infirmity was a hindrance to him who desired to be healed, now each hath power to approach, for now it is not an Angel that troubleth, it is the Lord of Angels who worketh all. The sick man cannot now say, 'while I am coming another steppeth down before me'; even if the whole world should come, the grace is not spent, the power is not exhausted, but remaineth equally great as it was before" (*On the Gospel According to St. John*, Homily 36).

The third sign—a healing on the Sabbath—is significant in the fullest sense, revealing the unity of work between the Father and the incarnate Son. And the Lord expounds the nature of that unity, using terms that show the distinction of the Father and the Son as Persons of the All-Holy Trinity.

"And therefore did the Jews persecute Jesus, and sought to slay Him, because He had done these things on the Sabbath day" (John 5:16). Breaking the Sabbath was a serious offense, punishable by death. Late rabbinic writings list a multitude of possible transgressions against this law.

"But Jesus answered them, My Father worketh hitherto, and I work" (v. 17). The Fathers consistently point out that, in spite of God's resting on the seventh day (Genesis 2:2), His providence and care for His creation never cease, and that the Lord's statement on this occasion refers specifically to that fact. Because of the Son's oneness with the Father, He works, too, even on the Sabbath day.

"Therefore the Jews sought the more to kill Him, because He not only had broken the Sabbath, but said also that God was His Father, making Himself equal with God" (v. 18). To the Jewish mind, this is the ultimate blasphemy. The Jews understand that Jesus is claiming to be God.

At this point the Evangelist begins to unveil the profound theological teachings of Jesus Christ concerning His relation to the Father. "Then answered Jesus and said unto them, Verily, I say unto you, The Son can do nothing of Himself, but what He seeth the Father do: for what things soever He doeth, these also doeth the Son likewise" (v. 19). It is by nature that "the Son can do nothing in opposition to the Father, nothing alien from, nothing strange to Him" (St. John Chrysostom, *On the Gospel According to St. John*, Homily 38).

"The Father loveth the Son, and showeth Him all things that Himself doeth; and He will show Him greater works than these" (v. 20). The word *love* gives us some idea of the inner life of the Holy Trinity.

Jesus indicates that the healing of the paralytic is only the beginning; there will be even greater works: not only will He cure, but He will also raise the dead. "For as the Father raiseth up the dead, and quickeneth them, even so the Son quickeneth whom He will" (v. 21). "He will" is not a contradiction to "can do nothing of Himself" but rather shows equality of power and authority. "You see therefore that 'cannot do anything of Himself' is the expression of One not taking away His (own) authority, but declaring the unvarying resemblance of His power and will (to those of the Father)" (St. John Chrysostom, ibid.).

"For the Father judgeth no man, but hath committed all judgment unto the Son" (v. 22). The idea expressed in this verse is completed in verse 27: "(The Father) hath given Him (the Son) authority to execute judgment also, because He is the Son of man." The Son is the agent of judgment because of His becoming man, but His judgment is not different from that of the Father. There is no doubt that the Jews fully understood Jesus' claims, and He knew that their anger was mounting. At the end of the chapter, He will tell them: "Do not think that I will accuse you to the Father: there is one that accuseth you, Moses, in whom ye trust. For had ye believed Moses, ye would have believed me: for he wrote of me" (vv. 45-46).

Jesus' use of the terms "given" and "sent" with reference to Himself does not in any way minimize His position, power, or authority. They are to be understood in the same way as "begotten," which in no way implies any temporal sequence. The statement in verse 26, for example, is tantamount to saying that the Son's "begotten-ness" includes His "having life in Himself." "For as the Father hath life in Himself, so hath He given to the Son to have life in Himself." That point is already established in the prologue to this Gospel: "in Him was life" (1:1).

Finally, hearing the word of the Son, one hears the voice of the Father, and believing in the Son is believing in the Father. "He that heareth my word, and believeth on Him that sent me, hath everlasting life, and shall not come into condemnation; but is passed from death into life...The hour is coming, and now is, when the dead shall hear the voice of the Son of God: and they that hear shall live" (vv. 24-25).

4

THE FOURTH SIGN: THE FEEDING OF THE FIVE THOUSAND (John 6:5-14)

The story of the feeding of the five thousand people, the fourth of the miraculous signs recorded by St. John, in his Gospel, is found also in the other three Gospels. In fact, this is the only miracle account that appears in all four (John 6:5-14; Matthew 14:15-21; Mark 6:34-44; and Luke 9:12-17).

There are some differences in the details reported by the Evangelists, but essentially they all tell the same story. As might be expected, St. John's narrative, written somewhat later than the others, not only relates the event itself, but it seems to offer a commentary on the theological significance of the miracle or sign. The kind of detail he includes leads us inevitably to this conclusion.

It should be noted also that, except for St. Luke, the Gospel writers saw fit to report the Lord's walking on the sea immediately after the miraculous feeding. But it was, so to speak, St. John's task to unify the two miracles in the sense that they contribute essential knowledge about the Person of our Lord Jesus Christ. As was the case in the preceding chapter, which dealt with the healing of the paralytic at the Sheep's Pool, the Lord gives His disciples a long discourse about Himself and His divine mission.

When St. John says, "After these things," he specifically refers to the healing of the paralytic and the discourse that follows in which He reveals to the Jews many things about His identity and His relation to the Father. The sentence continues, "He went over the sea of Galilee, which is the sea of Tiberias" (6:1). The people supposed that He had gone in a boat, as did His disciples, and they will ask Him later when He came to Capernaum (see 6:22). The mention of the name Tiberias probably reflects the rather later composition of the fourth Gospel, since in Jesus' time the lake seems not to have been known by this name.

The great multitude that followed Him, Galileans, were like the Jews described in the second chapter (v. 23), who "believed in His name when they saw the miracles which he did." But since Jesus "knew all men," that is, what is in their hearts and what motivates and impresses them, "He did not commit Himself to them" (v. 24), that is, He had no trust in their display of belief. As He already knew, many of those who were thus attracted to Him would leave Him later (6:66). Their interest in the miracle-worker waned when they heard His doctrine.

His going up into a mountain (6:3) in order to be with His disciples and to teach them recalls the opening of the Sermon on the Mount as recorded by St. Matthew (chs. 5-7). In that case He revealed Himself as the Divine Lawgiver, not like Moses, who was only able to convey what God revealed to him. In that Sermon, He makes some profound contrasts between the old Law and His new Law; in the same way, in the present case, He will reveal the insufficiency of the old Law.

"And the passover, a feast of the Jews, was nigh" (6:4). St. John Chrysostom finds the mention of the passover significant: " 'How then,' saith some one, 'doth He not go up to the feast, but when all are pressing to Jerusalem, goeth Himself into Galilee, and not Himself alone, but taketh His disciples with Him, and proceedeth thence to Capernaum?' Because henceforth He was quietly annulling the Law, taking occasion from the wickedness of the Jews" (*On the Gospel According to St. John*, Homily 42). Further, it seems that the reference to the nearness of the Passover sets the stage for the Lord's long discourse on the following day, in which He speaks of Himself as the "bread which came down from heaven." It may also strike some readers of the Gospel as strange that the Evangelist should have to identify the Passover as a "feast of the Jews." Could it indicate that at the time of the Gospel's composition the separation between the Synagogue and the Church was complete and that a considerable number of Christians, converts from paganism, would not immediately know what the Passover was?

"When Jesus then lifted up His eyes, and saw a great company come unto Him, He saith unto Philip, Whence shall we buy bread, that these may eat?" (6:5). While the other Evangelists indicate that it was the disciples who asked Jesus to send the people away so that they could buy provisions, St. John tells us that it was the Lord Himself who first asked how they were to be fed. If it is necessary to explain the difference, we might suggest that their request was probably in response to His question. In any event, the Lord's compassion toward the multitude, noted by the other Evangelists, is manifest here as well. But, in addition to His concern for the temporary satisfaction of their physical needs, we shall see, in the above-mentioned discourse, that He has a much deeper concern for their spiritual needs.

"When Jesus then lifted up His eyes, and saw a great company come unto Him, He saith unto Philip, Whence shall we buy bread, that these may eat?" (John 6:5). Jesus' immediate response to seeing the great company is His concern for their needs, expressed first in terms of physical needs. But, as will be evident later His real concern is for their spiritual well-being. In fact, in St. Mark's account of the same incident, it is noted that the Lord "was moved with compassion toward them, because they were as sheep not having a shepherd: and He began to teach them many things" (6:34). Also we should remember His invitation to the disciples, when the Samaritans approached: "Lift up your eyes, and look on the fields; for they are white already to harvest" (John 4:35). The fact is that the Samaritans, in coming to seek Him, were already disposed to believe on Him, not only because of the testimony of the woman who met Jesus at the well but also because they too were expecting "the Christ, the Saviour of the world" (4:42). The task of bringing the Galilean Jews to Him, who also had the prophets to predispose them to faith in Him, should have been easy for the disciples in view of what He said to them: "I sent you to reap that whereon ye bestowed no labour: Other men laboured, and ye are entered into their labours" (4:38). This great company, which will be fed miraculously, was undoubtedly made up of these Galilean Jews.

Jesus' question to Philip is explained: "And this He said to prove him: for He Himself knew what He would do" (John 6:6). Would Philip remember what Jesus had said when the disciples asked Him to eat of those provisions they had brought from the Samaritan city: "I have meat to eat that ye know not of" (John 4:32)? Had his faith in Jesus' power increased to the point where he could be sure that Jesus could feed them even if there were no provisions?

Apparently not: "Philip answered Him, Two hundred penny-worth of bread is not sufficient for them, that every one of them may take a little" (John 6:7). As to why the Lord had asked Philip and not someone else, St. John Chrysostom offers this explanation: "He knew which of His disciples needed most instruction; for this is he who afterwards said, 'Show us the Father, and it sufficeth us' (John 14:8), and on this account Jesus was beforehand bringing him into a proper state" (*On the Gospel According to St. John*, Homily 42). Philip would certainly be a witness to the sign of the feeding of the five thousand, yet his understanding would remain insufficient, as the question in Chapter 14 indicates.

There seems to be one ray of hope that the disciples might be beginning to understand something of the Lord's power in Andrew's calling attention to "a lad here, which hath five barley loaves and two small fishes..." but he fails to acknowledge that even with so little, Jesus could have fed so large a crowd. He goes on to say, "But what are they among so many?" (6:8-9).

It is only St. John who mentions that the loaves were of "barley," and it is not evident why, but it is known that such was characteristically the bread of the poor. Do the lad and what he had symbolize anything? In any event, it should be taken into consideration that the Lord literally multiplied what was offered by this lad in order to feed the whole hungry multitude.

"And Jesus said, Make the men to sit down. Now there was much grass in the place. So the men sat down in number about five thousand" (6:10). (The word translated "sit" and "sat down" is literally "reclined," as people were accustomed to do at a banquet.) In spite of the disciples' helplessness and their practical considerations as to the insufficiency of the bread and the fish, their obedience to Him is constant, for they did exactly as He commanded.

The other Evangelists' record of the event include the Lord's telling the disciples to feed them: "Give ye them to eat," for example in St. Luke's Gospel (9:13). St. John Chrysostom emphasizes the disciples' obedience in these terms: "The same men, who at first disbelieved so much as to say,

'Whence shall we buy bread?' began so far to believe even before they saw the miracle, that they readily made the multitude to sit down." (ibid.).

In light of the fact that the "passover was nigh," and of the discourse on the significance of the miracle/sign which the Lord delivered on the following day, it is possible to see in the details of the narrative a great deal of symbolism. "Jesus took the loaves; and when He had given thanks, He distributed to the disciples, and the disciples to them that were set down, and likewise of the fishes as much as they would" (6:11). The procedure is typical of the Jewish meal: the taking of the bread, the giving thanks, and breaking it (implied also in St. John's use of "distributed"). In the institution of the Eucharist, the same words are used, and it is not inappropriate to see here a figure of that very supper. For, although the multitude will be filled physically, it is by means of the miracle. The miracle of the Lord's giving his own body and blood to fill mankind's deepest hunger, communion with God, may be said to be symbolized in this preliminary "supper."

"When they were filled, He said unto His disciples: Gather up the fragments that remain, that nothing be lost. Therefore they gathered them together, and filled twelve baskets with the fragments of the five barley loaves, which remained over and above unto them that had eaten" (John 6:12-13). Here we have one of the clearest demonstrations of the Lord's power over all things: He multiplied the bread in sufficient quantity to satisfy the five thousand and to fill exactly twelve baskets. This fact is likewise evidence that the miracle was not simply a show of His power, but that it pointed to some significant purpose or plan of His.

The number of baskets, obviously, corresponded to the number of the Apostles, and would serve as convincing proof to them that the feeding was no illusion but a reality. Further, as will be made increasingly clear as the Gospel story progresses, these same chosen disciples will be made the instruments whereby the human race can eat of the miraculous Bread, which is Christ Himself. For, in the person of Simon Peter, the Apostles will be commissioned to feed His flock (see 21:15-17).

The Lord's words, His brief explanation of why they were to gather up the fragments, "that nothing be lost," deserves some comment. These words are repeated later on the following day in the Lord's discourse at the point where He speaks of the will of the Father, "that of all which He hath given me I should lose nothing." Again, in the high priestly prayer just before His crucifixion, He says: "While I was with them in the world, I kept them in thy name: those that thou gavest me I have kept, and none of them is lost, but the son of perdition; that the Scripture (Psalm 109/110:8) might be fulfilled" (John 17:2). Judas was still one of the twelve, and one basket of fragments must have been his. Does this mean that he was not yet determined to betray the Lord? And, the Lord's will was that none be lost. St. John Chrysostom offers this explanation of how Judas was lost: "And in another place He saith, 'Of all that thou gavest me, I will surely lose nothing' (v. 39). Yet not only was he (the traitor Judas) lost, but many afterwards; how then saith He, 'I will in nowise lose?' 'For my part, I will not lose.' So in another place, declaring the matter more clearly, He said, 'I will in nowise cast out' (v. 37). 'Not through any fault of mine, not because I either instigate or abandon them; but if they start away of themselves, I draw them not by necessity' ('I will not force them')" (*On the Gospel According to St. John,* Homily 81).

"Then those men, when they had seen the miracle that Jesus did, said, This is of a truth that Prophet that should come into the world. When Jesus therefore perceived that they would come and take Him by force, to make Him a king, He departed again into a mountain Himself alone" (6:14-15).

That the Israelites expected "the Prophet" to come is plain from the question of John the Baptist's disciples (Matthew 11:3) and from that of the priests and Levites sent by the Jews (John 1:21). That Prophet had certainly been foretold: "The Lord thy God will raise up unto thee a Prophet from the midst of thee, of thy brethren, like unto me; unto him ye shall hearken" (Deuteronomy 18:15, 18; see also Genesis 49:10; Isaiah 7:14 and 9:6). It is worthy of note that in this chapter of Deuteronomy, in verse 15, the Lord says, "like unto me" and in verse 18, "like unto thee." That the men who had been fed miraculously should conclude that Jesus was that Prophet because of the miracle itself gives an indication of the kind of Prophet they wanted: one who could benefit them materially.

The Lord Jesus was born to be king; we know this from His answer to Pilate (John 18:37; Luke 23:2), and from the testimony of the Angel to the all-holy Virgin (Luke 1:32-33). His kingdom, however, is not of this world (John 18:36), and He rejected any attempt to make Him king in any worldly sense. So He left and went up to a mountain to be alone.

Then, there follows in the narration, as we have already noted, another miracle: Jesus' walking on the sea and His enabling the disciples to reach land in spite of the storm that had come up. We see in this, first, that the people had observed that Jesus had not got into the boat with His disciples; yet when they came to Capernaum, they saw Him there, and thus, they could not help but inquire as to when and how He got there. Just as He could feed more than five thousand people from five loaves and two fish, He is also able to cross over the water without the aid of a boat.

Several details are important in this part of the narration, important and obviously intentional on the part of the Evangelist: that the disciples' fear came from the fact that it was dark and that Jesus was absent. This seems to point to the human condition resulting from the absence of the illumination of Him who is the light of the world. Further, the Lord's declaration, "I am" (not "It is I," as most translations have it), the name of God Himself, is intended to reveal His identity to His disciples. God is with them, and there is no reason to be afraid: "The Lord is my light and my salvation, of whom then shall I be afraid" (Psalm 26/27:1). His revelation of Himself at this point as the One who has dominion over all things both explains the miraculous things that have happened and sets the stage for the discourse on the following day.

5

THE FIFTH SIGN: THE BLIND MAN
(John 9:1-38)

The healing of the man born blind is the fifth of the Lord's signs recorded in the Gospel of St. John. Like the others, this one points to the Person and work of Jesus Christ: His divinity, His unity with the Father, His being the promised and expected Messiah, and His mission or purpose in His coming in the flesh. The miracle is unique in several respects, and particular stress is given to His work as a "new creation."

In the temple, at the feast of Tabernacles, the Lord had declared that He is the only source of the living, or life-creating, water (7:37-38); that He is "the light of the world" (8:12); that He was sent by the Father (8:16); that the Jews who failed to recognize Him were not true descendants of Abraham (8:39); and that He is God: "Before Abraham was, I am" (8:58). This, then, is the context for the present sign: Jesus escapes from the Jews who seek to kill Him (8:59), leaves the temple, and immediately performs a work that demonstrates the truth of all that He claimed to be. He causes a blind man to see and imparts something else much greater besides—spiritual sight.

St. John tells us that "as Jesus passed by, He saw a man which was blind from birth" (9:1). The Evangelist does not say that the blind man was brought to Jesus, as was the case in the incident recorded in St. Mark 8:27 and 10:46, or that the blind man himself approached Jesus, asking for mercy, as we find in the healings in St. Matthew 9:27 and 20:30. It is clear that in this case, Jesus Himself took the initiative.

The dialogue that follows between the disciples and Jesus (9:2-3) clears up a misconception that was common at that time. "Master, who did sin, this man, or his parents, that he was born blind? Jesus answered, Neither hath this man, nor his parents: but that the work of God should be made manifest in him." There is no doubt that the Lord does not mean absolutely that neither the man nor his parents had sinned, for no one is without sin. He insists rather that the blindness was not a consequence of the sins of either. (See Augustine, *On the Gospel of St. John*, Tractate 44, and St. John Chrysostom, *On the Gospel According to St. John*, Homily 56, no. 1.)

The juxtaposition of "neither hath this man sinned, nor his parents" and "but that the works of God should be made manifest in Him," has caused no little difficulty for interpreters. "Some say that this conjunction is not at all expressive of cause, but related to the consequence of the miracle" (St. John Chrysostom, ibid.). That is, it is not specifically so that the miracle could be performed that the man was born blind. The emphasis seems to be rather on the fact that, since the Lord finds a man in such a condition, He chooses to use him and the condition for the miraculous work that would manifest God's glory. Further, He perceives the man's response beforehand.

To return to the Lord's answer to His disciples: anyone familiar with the Scriptures might have remembered that the notion that a person's affliction is necessarily God's punishment is refuted by the Book of Job. The Lord Himself denies the connection between sins and divine punishment in another case (Luke 13:1-5). The disciples' question undoubtedly reflected the popular superstition. Whatever may have been the cause of this man's blindness, the important thing is how Jesus will turn affliction into a manifestation of God's work, glory, and power.

Jesus then says: "I must work the works of Him that sent me, while it is day: the night cometh, when no man can work. As long as I am in the world, I am the light of the world" (9:4-5). The Son of God is the light of the world. His work on coming into the world is to enlighten every man (John 1:9). He must do this "while it is day," that is, as long as He is in the world (9:5). The "night that cometh, when no man can work" (9:4) is that time when Christ will be delivered up by sinful men who prefer the darkness and He will go away. Note, later in this Gospel, the time of Jesus' betrayal: "And it was night" (13:30); at His crucifixion, "darkness fell over the whole earth" (Luke 23:44). By those who believe, He is still seen—through the eyes of faith and by the operation of the Holy Spirit. Followers of Christ are thus admonished to make use of the day in working out their salvation, for the night of their death will come when they will no longer be able to work.

When Jesus had spoken briefly to His disciples about His work in the world, "He spat on the ground, and made clay of the spittle, and He anointed the eyes of the blind man with the clay" (John 9:6). It may be noted here that St. Mark records two occasions when Jesus effected healings by the use of spittle (7:33 and 8:23).

The dust of the ground, water (in the form of spittle), a man—references to these should recall to our minds the early chapters of Genesis. The eternal Word of God, now incarnate, who created man from dust after watering the whole earth (Genesis 2:5-7), here performs another act of creation—a re-creation. The power of the Word, proceeding from His mouth, "the same both formed the man and opened his eyes" (St. John Chrysostom, *On the Gospel According to St. John*, Homily 58). The "new creation" (2 Corinthians 5:17) is initiated by Christ, who has just called Himself "the light of the world" (v. 5). The works of God will be made manifest in the blind man, who will first receive his physical sight.

"And He said unto him, Go, wash in the pool of Siloam, (which is by interpretation, Sent). He went his way therefore, and washed, and came seeing" (v. 7). Obviously, the Lord could give the man sight by a word or even simply by the exercise of His will. He chooses instead another way that at first strikes us as extraordinary.

Two things claim our attention as Jesus sends the man to be washed in Siloam. Remember, first, that Jesus had been in the temple at the Feast of Tabernacles. Part of that feast involved bringing a large urn of water from Siloam on the first seven days—but not the eighth—for rites of purification. These rites were a figure of the true purification, which is in Christ. "By sending him to Siloam, He desires to prove that He is not estranged from the Law and the Old Covenant" (St. John Chrysostom, ibid.). There is further significance to the use of water from Siloam during a festival to commemorate the Hebrews' desert wanderings. This water recalls the water that came out of the rock of Horeb when, by God's command, it was struck by Moses (Exodus 17:1-6).

When we consider the Apostle Paul's explanation of that rock, it becomes clear why the Lord directs the blind man to wash in Siloam. "All our fathers...were baptized from heaven; and did all drink the same spiritual drink; for they drank of that spiritual Rock that followed them: and that Rock was Christ" (1 Corinthians 10:4; see Exodus 15:16 and Numbers 20:11).

The second remarkable thing is that the Evangelist John emphasizes the meaning of the name "Siloam," which is "Sent."

Jesus repeatedly refers to His own being sent, so much so that we could call Him the "Sent One." The pool, then, stands for Christ, and being washed in the pool is being washed in Christ. It is a direct figure of baptism. Compare the words of St. Paul: "As many of you as have been baptized into Christ have put on Christ" (Galatians 3:27).

The remainder of St. John 9 traces the blind man's spiritual progress. St. John Chrysostom describes his behavior in the face of repeated questioning by the people and the Pharisees as one of calm assurance, unperturbed by the evident malice of the latter. "When thou didst open the eyes of him who could not see the perceptible light, thou didst enlighten the eyes of his soul as well. Thou didst move him to glorify thee, for he had come to know thee as the Creator, who out of compassion didst appear as a mortal man" (Matins, Canon, Ode 5, Wednesday of the Blind Man).

The man born blind goes from the bare knowledge of what has happened to him—"A man that is called Jesus made clay, and anointed mine eyes, and said unto me, Go to the pool of Siloam, and wash: and I went and washed, and I received sight" (v. 11)—to a complete conviction about the identity of his Benefactor. When he is brought to the Pharisees, and they question him, he offers the same simple history (v. 15). During that interview, the rulers conclude that Jesus could not possibly "be of God, because He keepeth not the Sabbath day" (v. 16). They ask the man born blind what he thinks of Jesus. Perhaps because he is emboldened by the division among the Pharisees or, more likely, because he is beginning to understand something about the man who healed him, he answers, "He is a prophet" (v. 17).

The Jewish leaders attempt to discredit the miracle, calling the man's parents to testify. "Is this your son, who ye say was born blind?" they are asked (v. 19). His parents affirm that he is their son, and that he was born blind. But they do not attempt to answer the third part of the question: "How then doth he now see?" They suggest instead that the leaders ask him directly, seeing that he is of age. "Blindness befell those who supposedly had eyes that saw, for darkness seized their minds and souls and enshrouded their thoughts when they beheld the man who was blind regain sight" (Matins, Aposticha sticheron, Monday of the Blind Man).

The man's parents avoid attributing his cure to Jesus, because they fear being "put out of the synagogue" (John 9:22).

In the Pharisees' eyes, Jesus' sin is double: works of healing and kneading, even though it be a salve, violated their Sabbath laws. Despite this "evidence" of Jesus' sinfulness, the young man refuses to call Him a sinner and restates what he knows: "Whereas I was blind, now I see" (v. 25).

The Jews call the man for a second encounter, and here we see that his conversion had already begun. The leaders are now almost obliged to acknowledge the miracle, but they remain determined to make the man deny that Jesus had anything to do with it. It is as if they are saying, "All right, you now have your sight, but you cannot give this man credit, because he is a sinner, so 'give God the praise'" (v. 24).

It is when they ask him to tell again how he received his sight that he appears ready to declare himself a disciple. "Wherefore would ye hear it again, will ye *also* be his disciples?" (v. 27, emphasis added).

They disparage the Lord and "revile" Him, but this serves only to increase the man's conviction that his Healer is "of God." The Jewish leaders declare him to be Jesus' disciple while they, proudly, are Moses'. They say they "know not whence He is," but that is a lie. Everyone seems to have known where the Lord was from (John 7:27). In another sense, of course, they speak the truth, because they do not know of His "coming down from heaven."

The man born blind is inspired to deliver a thoroughly theological rebuttal to the theologians. The truly miraculous thing, he suggests, is that they, who know the things that pertain to God, do not know where Jesus is from, when God had obviously heard Him. The man's conclusion: the One who gave him sight is both a worshipper of God and a man who does His will. He has done something never done before: "He opened the eyes of one that was born blind" (vv. 30-32). He has "to be of God" (v. 33).

Their only recourse was to fall back on the old superstition, that his affliction was due to his parents' or his own sins. "Thou wast altogether born in sins, and dost thou teach us?" They realize that the man confesses Jesus to be the Christ; true to their threat, they cast him out (v. 34).

"Jesus heard that they had cast him out; and when He had found him, He said unto him, Dost thou believe on the Son of God? He answered and said, Who is he, Lord, that I might believe on Him? And Jesus said unto him, Thou hast both seen Him, and it is He that talketh with thee" (vv. 35-37).

St. John Chrysostom has this to say about the Lord's finding him: "The Jews cast him out from the Temple, and the Lord of the Temple found him; he was separated from that pestilent company, and met with the fountain of salvation; he was dishonored by those who dishonored Christ, and was honored by the Lord of angels...He made Himself known to him who before knew Him not, and enrolled him in the company of His own disciples." The young man's expression—"Who is He?"—is that of "a longing and inquiring soul. He knoweth not Him in whose defense he had spoken so much" (*On John*, Homily 59, no. 1).

"And he said, Lord, I believe. And he worshipped Him" (v. 38). Again, St. John Chrysostom says: "And then the man, showing his great earnestness, straightway worshipped; which few of those who were healed had done; as, for instance, the lepers, and some others; by this act declaring His divine power. For that no one might think that what had been said by him was a mere expression, he added also the deed" (ibid.).

Thus, this story of illumination, at first physical but later spiritual as well, is completed. Having received such an unheard of miracle and, no doubt, in view of the envy of the Jews, the man has begun to perceive that his Healer is some extraordinary person. He ventures to call Him a prophet. Then, undoubtedly inspired, he defends Him theologically and is ready to be His disciple. When he is found by Jesus, he is ready to believe that He is the Son of God, and he worships Him.

The whole narration of St. John 9 shows adequately enough that this miracle is a sign, but the last three verses underscore its meaning and application. When Jesus says, "For judgment I am come into this world" (v. 39), He does not contradict what is recorded in the previous chapter: "I judge no man" (8:15). He is telling us that His very presence is a judgment, and those who should have known Him but rejected Him condemn themselves. He had explained this already in His conversation with Nicodemus: "And this is the condemnation, that light is come into the world, and men loved darkness rather than the light, because their deeds were evil" (3:19). The consequences of His presence are spelled out in the second part of v. 39: "that they which see not might see; and that they which see might be made blind."

To the question of the Pharisees who were with Him, "Are we blind also?" He answers, "If ye were blind, ye should have no sin; but now ye say, We see; therefore your sin remaineth" (vv. 40, 41). St. Augustine explains this saying in a paraphrase: " 'If ye were blind,' that is, if ye considered yourselves blind, if ye called yourselves blind, ye also would have recourse to the physician: if then in this way 'ye were blind, ye

should have no sin;' for I am come to take away sin. 'But now
ye say, We see; therefore your sin remaineth.' Why? Because
by saying, 'We see,' ye seek not the physician, and ye remain
in your blindness" (*On the Gospel of St. John*, Tractate 44).

6

THE SIXTH SIGN: THE RAISING OF LAZARUS
(John 11:1-45)

The resurrection of Lazarus, the story of which occupies almost the entire eleventh chapter of St. John's Gospel, is the
sixth of the Lord's signs. Keep in mind that "signs" are not
simply demonstrations of His power but revelations of the
truth about His Person and His work. The raising of Lazarus is
the ultimate sign, offering the clearest evidence of who Christ
is and of His purpose in the world.

The liturgical texts for the Saturday of the holy and righteous Lazarus, the day before the Lord's triumphal entry into
Jerusalem, repeatedly emphasize several points: the reality of
the Incarnation and of the two natures in Christ, His power
over death, the foretelling of His own death and resurrection,
and the assurance of the resurrection of those who believe in
Him.

"Now a certain man was sick, named Lazarus, of Bethany,
the town of Mary and Martha" (11:1). We know of these sisters from an incident recorded in St. Luke's Gospel (10:38-
42), in which the Lord visits their house "in a certain village."
We have had no information about their brother Lazarus until
now. Attempts to identify him with the Lazarus who was laid
at the rich man's gate (Luke 16:20) have not been convincing.

"It was that Mary which anointed the Lord with ointment,
and wiped His feet with her hair, whose brother Lazarus was

sick" (11:2; see 12:3). There are records of two other anoint-
ings of the Lord, one in the house of Simon the leper (Matthew
26:7 and Mark 14:3) and another in the house of Simon the
Pharisee (Luke 7:37). The woman in the first is called simply
"a woman with an alabaster box of very precious ointment" or
"spikenard"; the woman in St. Luke's Gospel is "a woman of
the city, which was a sinner." Despite certain similarities, we
have to conclude that in the Synoptics there were two different
persons who anointed the Lord. Mary, the sister of Lazarus, is
a third woman-anointer. Attempts to identify her with either of
the other two seem to have been made in early times, as St.
John Chrysostom (fourth century) roundly rejects any such
identification. He points out that Mary was never described as
a sinful woman, that the anointing took place apparently in her
own home, and that Jesus knew and loved all three, the sisters
and their brother: they were certainly friends and perhaps disciples (*On the Gospel According to St. John*, Homily 62).

"Therefore his sisters sent unto Him, saying, Lord, behold, he
whom thou lovest is sick" (11:3). Since they sent someone else, it
appears that they simply wanted to inform Him. There is no indication that they were asking Him to come to heal their brother.

"When Jesus heard that, He said, This sickness is not unto
death, but for the glory of God, that the Son of God might be glorified thereby" (11:4). "Observe how He again asserts that His
glory and the Father's is One," St. John Chrysostom says (ibid.).
Note also what the saint says about the connective word *that*: "It
denotes not cause, but consequence; the sickness happened from
other causes, but He used it for the glory of God." Even when
the sisters had heard from the messenger that the Lord had
said, "This sickness is not unto death," and then seeing him
dead, they did not lose their trust in Jesus. This is evident in the
way they received Him when He arrived. It should also be
noted that "being glorified" may mean "being praised," but in

Jesus' case, it means something quite different: that He might save mankind by His own suffering and crucifixion.

"Now Jesus loved Martha, and her sister, and Lazarus" (11:5). That sickness should befall a good person or one whom the Lord loves should cause no dismay, for "whom the Lord loveth He chasteneth" (Hebrews 12:6).

"When He had heard therefore that he was sick, He abode two days still in the same place where He was" (11:5). "Wherefore tarried He? that Lazarus might breathe his last, and be buried; that none might be able to assert that He restored him when not yet dead, saying that it was a lethargy, a fainting, a fit, but not death. On this account, He tarried so long, that corruption began, and they said, 'he now stinketh'" (St. John Chrysostom, ibid.). Could it not also be that since the resurrection of Lazarus was to be a figure or type of the Lord's own resurrection, in which He proved to be "the resurrection and the life," His coming to Lazarus on "the third day" reinforces the figurative nature of the event?

"Then after that saith He to His disciples, Let us go into Judea again" (11:7). The unusual thing here is that the Lord did not always tell His disciples where He was going. Perhaps if their fear was too great, they might abandon Him, or, He was sensitive to their frightened state. Note that He speaks of Judea and not specifically of Bethany. He is returning to the place of His rejection.

Jesus' disciples question the wisdom of His intention: "Master, the Jews of late sought to stone thee; and goest thou thither again?" (John 11:8). Did they fear only for the Lord's safety or their own? St. John Chrysostom raises this question and, characteristically, defends the disciples, for "they were not yet perfect," implying here, as he says elsewhere, that they must be judged on the basis of what they did after they were perfected.

The Lord's answer, which they probably did not fully understand, is related to the total picture of His work and is apparently designed to prepare them for the shock of all the things that they will see Him undergo in Jerusalem. "Are there not twelve hours in the day? If any man walk in the day, he stumbleth not, because He seeth the light of this world" (11:9). Jesus refers to His own presence in the world as day, His day. As long as He is in the world, He is the light of the world (9:4-5). His hour has not yet come, and this is a kind of assurance that no harm can come to Him or to them, as long as they are with Him.

"But if a man walk in the night he stumbleth because there is no light in him" (11:10). Even if it is really night, those who have the light of Christ will not stumble; but on the other hand, those who do not have that light will stumble at high noon. There is a reminiscence of Isaiah's assessment of Israel's plight, the result of her sinfulness, in this. "Therefore is judgment far from us, neither doth justice overtake us: we wait for light, but behold obscurity; for brightness, but we walk in darkness. We grope for the wall like the blind, and we grope as if we had no eyes: we stumble at noon day as in the night: we are in desolate places like the dead" (Isaiah 59:9-10). To those who do not believe, Christ, and especially His cross, will be a "stumbling-block" (1 Corinthians 1:23, also 1 Peter 2:6-8 and Romans 9:31-33).

Jesus assures the disciples that it is not yet to confront the Jews that He will go. "These things said He: and after that He saith unto them, Our friend Lazarus sleepeth; but I go; that I may awake him out of sleep" (11:11). The disciples misunderstand and offer another reason not to go: if Lazarus is but sleeping, there is nothing urgent to demand the Lord's presence. "Then said His disciples, Lord, if he sleep, he shall do well. Howbeit Jesus spake of his death; but they thought that

He had spoken of taking rest in sleep. Then said Jesus unto them plainly, Lazarus is dead" (11:12-14). The disciples must have thought at first that it was strange to go such a distance merely to wake Lazarus up. (Among later Christians, "asleep in the Lord" became the common way of referring to a believer's death. The English word *cemetery* is derived from the Greek *koimeterion*, a "sleeping-place.")

"And I am glad for your sakes that I was not there, to the intent ye may believe; nevertheless let us go unto him" (11:15). He knows of Lazarus' death, even without being there, and He explains why He is glad. We may understand from this that the Lord considered it vital for the disciples to have an unwavering faith, in view of the work He would send them to do. If He had been there, He could have responded to the sisters' earnest plea to heal their brother.

"Then said Thomas, which is called Didymus, unto his fellow-disciples, Let us also go, that we may die with Him" (11:16). Thomas' impetuous proposal has been understood in a variety of ways. It may express his fear for the Lord and for himself, showing that as yet he had no idea of the Lord's real power. St. John Chrysostom calls it an expression of cowardice but goes on to point out the contrast between Thomas' present feeling and his heroic conviction after the resurrection. In another way, Thomas' proposal turns out to be a prophetic exhortation: Jesus' death is unique in that He dies for all mankind, and yet everyone who follows Him will share in His death. (See St. Paul's explanation in Romans 6:1-11.)

"Then when Jesus came, He found that he had lain in the grave four days already" (11:17). A common belief was that the spirit hovers over the body for three days. The Evangelist draws our attention to the time that has passed since Lazarus' burial so that no one might imagine that the resurrection of Lazarus was a kind of reanimation. Lazarus had not just died, as was the case with Jairus' daughter (Mark 5:35). Corruption has set in. Christ the Life will give life to one who was really and verifiably dead.

"Now Bethany was nigh unto Jerusalem, about fifteen furlongs off" (11:18). Bethany was not only where Lazarus was; the city was to figure in the last days before the crucifixion, and the Lord lodged there after His triumphal entry into Jerusalem.

When Martha heard that the Lord was coming, she went out to meet Him, and she expressed her faith in His power to heal and prevent death: "If thou hadst been here, my brother had not (would not have) died" (11:21). She adds that "even now, whatsoever thou wilt ask of God, He will give it thee" (v. 22), but it does not seem that she is asking for her brother's return to life. This seems even less likely in light of the exchange that follows. The Lord assures her that Lazarus will rise again. She understands him to speak of "the resurrection at the last day" (v. 23, 24).

It is then that Jesus states that that future resurrection is already present in His Person: "I am the resurrection and the life" (v. 25). He Himself is the source and essence of resurrection and life. What all the previous signs signified comes to its climax as Jesus faces death in the person of Lazarus and defeats it.

Responding to the Lord's declaration of power to give life to both the dead and the living (vv. 25-26), Martha makes a three-fold confession of the truth about the Lord's identity: He is the Christ, or Messiah; He is the Son of God; and He is the Redeemer whose coming into the world was promised (v. 27).

When Mary is informed of His presence, she goes quickly to Him and expresses what her sister has already said about the Lord's power to heal (vv. 28-32).

"When Jesus therefore saw her weeping, and the Jews also weeping which came with her, He groaned in the spirit, and was troubled" (v. 33). The Lord's reaction to their grief is understood by the Fathers in at least three ways: He is displeased at their lack of faith; He represses His own grief; or He, the Life itself, expresses the divine displeasure at the very phenomenon of death. He created man for life, and sin had brought about death.

Jesus' humanity is given full expression in the next two verses (34-35). He asks where they have laid him. And He weeps. As the all-knowing God, of course, He not only knows where Lazarus is buried but also knows that He will turn grief into joy.

The Jews' reaction is two-fold: they are impressed by the deepness of Jesus' love for His friend (v. 36), and they wonder why One who had done such great wonders had not prevented Lazarus' death (v. 37).

The "groaning" within Himself (which is the same as "groaned in the spirit") of verse 33 is repeated here (v. 38); so we are inclined to accept the third of its possible meanings.

Jesus tells them to remove the stone from the entrance to the burial cave. Martha protests that corruption has begun (v. 39). The Lord reminds her that He has already told her that if she believes, she will see the glory of God (v. 40).

To show His oneness with the Father, that His own power was also the Father's, and that He was sent by the Father, Jesus prays, as He says, so that the bystanders might understand (v. 41-42).

Then "He cried with a loud voice, Lazarus, come forth. And he that was dead came forth, bound hand and foot with grave-clothes: and his face was bound about with a napkin. Jesus saith unto them, Loose him and let him go" (vv. 43-44). Thus the ultimate sign is carried out: the Life has given life to one who was dead. The Lord establishes the truth about His mission to destroy the finality of death; He affirms the general resurrection; and He prepares them for His own.

When He says, "Lazarus, come forth," it is evident that He Himself has the power to raise the dead. It is also apparent that His earlier assertion that "the hour is coming, when the dead shall hear the voice of the Son of God, and they that hear shall live," now takes place (John 5:28). Lazarus' coming forth still bound with grave-clothes is not less miraculous, and seems to have a definite purpose. By carrying out His command to "loose him," others would touch Lazarus and be able to bear witness to the reality of his resurrection.

The reaction of the authorities is predictable: they fear for the security of the nation (vv. 47-48). They plot to have Jesus put to death, and the high priest unwittingly prophesies that Jesus will die not only on behalf of Israel but for all people (vv. 49-52). He scarcely imagined that Jesus' death would destroy death itself and make it possible for not only the chosen people but for all people to have salvation and eternal life.

7

FINAL COMMENTS ON SECTIONS I AND II

We have arranged our treatment of the Lord's miracles according to the order in which they appear in the Orthodox Church's lectionary. The first part dealt with those that are contained in the Gospel lessons appointed to be read on the Sundays of the thirty-two weeks after Pentecost. In the course of our study, it seemed appropriate to explore the meaning of the whole period and the place that the miracles occupy in it.

In a sense, the "after Pentecost" season corresponds to the experience of the Church immediately after the descent of the Holy Spirit, when the Church was born and its mission to the world was initiated. The Church must carry out the "great commission": "Go ye therefore, and make disciples of all nations, baptizing them in the name of the Father, and of the Son, and of the Holy Spirit: teaching them to observe all things whatsoever I have commanded you, and, lo, I am with you always, unto the consummation of the age" (Matthew 28:20, translation adjusted to correspond more exactly with the original). The Acts of the Apostles, the New Testament book that immediately follows the four Gospels, is the record of this work.

Part and parcel of the apostolic preaching of Christ was the attestation of eye-witnesses, the Apostles themselves, to the Savior's miracles. In St. Peter's first sermon, at the Feast of Pentecost, he refers specifically to the "miracles and wonders and signs which God did by Him (Christ) in the midst of you (the Jews), as ye yourselves know" (Acts 2:24) as proof of His identity and of His divine mission. The proclamation of Christ cannot omit His miracles.

In the second section, we treated the signs recorded by the fourth evangelist, St. John. The accounts of these signs—excepting the sixth, the resurrection of Lazarus—are read as Gospel lessons during the period after Holy Pascha, the forty days before the Lord's ascension into heaven. The first sign, the changing of water into wine at the marriage feast in Cana of Galilee (2:1-11), is the lesson for Monday of the Second Week of Pascha (as well as for the rite of matrimony); the second sign, the healing of the nobleman's son (4:46-54), is read on Monday of the Third Week; the third sign, the healing of the paralytic at the Sheep's Pool in "Bethesda" (5:1-15), is read on the Fourth Sunday of Pascha; the fourth sign, the feeding of the five thousand (6:5-14), is read on Wednesday of the Fifth Week; the fifth sign, the giving of sight to the man born blind (9:1-38), is read on the Sixth Sunday. The story of Lazarus' being raised from the dead (11:1-45) is the theme of the Saturday before Palm Sunday. It is regarded not only as a real event but also as a sign of the Lord's own resurrection and the general resurrection.

Again, this period corresponds to the experience of the early Church: once the catechumens are baptized at Pascha, they are further instructed in the doctrine of the Lord Jesus Christ, the transforming power of His presence in the "signs," and the continuation of that presence in the holy mysteries. St. Cyril of Jerusalem, in his *Catechetical Lectures*, calls attention to the fact that these post-baptismal teachings are designed to explore the deep meaning of the holy mysteries that the newly baptized received at Pascha.

In the Fourth Gospel, attendant details or circumstances and accompanying discourses or elucidations demonstrate that the miracles are indeed signs of the truth about Jesus Christ and His identity and purpose. Some of these details and explanations are not included in the synoptic accounts of certain miracles. And St. John includes miracles that the other Gospel writers do not (the miracle at Cana of Galilee and the raising of Lazarus). It is perhaps not too bold to state that St. John had advantages. He was a later writer, and he had experienced perhaps two generations of life in the Church, the body of Christ. He was thus able to see more clearly the theological implications of the events and wondrous things contained in the three earlier Gospels.

The third section of this survey will look at miracles, signs and wonders that are not included in the two categories already considered. Some of these also appear in the lectionary throughout the year, and that will be noted. In the following chapters we shall study those miracles that are recorded in St. Mark's Gospel.

III

1

THE HEALING OF A POSSESSED MAN (Mark 1)

The Holy Gospel of St. Mark begins with a simple title: "The beginning of the Gospel of Jesus Christ, the Son of God" (1:1). There is neither an account of the Lord's birth nor a genealogy of His ancestors according to the flesh. We find those only in the Gospels of St. Matthew and St. Luke.

St. Mark continues with quotations from the prophecies of Malachi (3:1) and Isaiah (40:3) that foretell the appearance of the Lord's Forerunner, and he identifies John (called "the Baptist") as that messenger (vv. 2-3).

There follows a brief description of the work and the preaching of the Baptist: "John did baptize in the wilderness, and preach the baptism of repentance for the remission of sins" (v. 4). We read of the response of the people of Jerusalem and all Judea to his preaching (v. 5), and we get a glimpse of his ascetic way of life as the authentication of his proclamation (v. 6). He is seen declaring, in extreme humility, that he is only the Precursor whose purpose is to prepare the way of "One mightier" than he (v. 7) and to reveal something of the nature of the mission of the Messiah (v. 8).

Verses 9-11 describe the Lord's baptism. The exchange between Jesus and John, familiar to us from Matthew 3:14-15, is not included here. Most importantly, St. Mark does give an account of the manifestation of the Holy Trinity: "the Spirit, descending like a dove," and the Father's "voice from heaven, saying, Thou art my beloved Son, in whom I am well pleased." St. Matthew and St. Luke record what happened as the Lord came up out of the water in practically identical terms; St. John the Evangelist records only the Baptist's testimony to what he had witnessed.

The temptation by Satan in the wilderness is briefly described (vv. 12-13), without the details available in St. Matthew and St. Luke. Then we find a short summary of the Lord's preaching (vv. 14-15). The most notable thing here is that Jesus repeats the proclamation of John the Baptist, "Repent, for the kingdom of heaven is at hand" (Matthew 3:2). Jesus' preaching authenticates the Baptist's role as Forerunner.

Jesus calls four of His disciples, Simon (Peter) and Andrew, and then James and John, the Sons of Zebedee. "And straightway they forsook their nets, and followed Him...and they left their father Zebedee...and went after Him." After this we find the Lord, accompanied by His disciples, teaching in the Synagogue at Capernaum (vv. 16-22).

The rest of the chapter gives us an account of the Lord's early miracles. These were healings—of a man possessed of an "unclean spirit," of Peter's mother, who was "sick of a fever," of "all that were diseased, and them that were possessed with devils," and of a leper.

The first miracle is described thus: "And there was in their synagogue a man with an unclean spirit, and he cried out saying, Let us alone; what have we to do with thee, thou Jesus of Nazareth? art thou come to destroy us? I know thee who thou art, the Holy One of God. And Jesus rebuked him, saying, Hold thy peace, and come out of him. And when the unclean spirit had torn him, and cried with a loud voice, he came out of him" (vv. 23-26).

The Blessed Theophylact captures the significance of this miracle: "The evil spirits are called unclean because they wickedly take pleasure in every kind of shameful deed. Moreover, the demon considers his departure from the man to be his own destruction; for the demons are without pity and believe that they suffer ill if they are not permitted to do evil to men. Also, because they love the flesh and are accustomed to feeding upon carnal vapors, they are starved when they do not dwell within a body. This is why the Lord says that the demons come out of a man by fasting (Mark 9:9). The foul demon did not say, 'Thou art holy,' for there were also many prophets who were holy. Instead he said, 'The Holy One,' with the article; that is, He who alone and by definition is Holy. But Christ shut his mouth in order to teach us that even if the demons speak the truth we must curb them. (Truth having no need of recommendation by the evil spirits.) The demon throws the man down and rends him so that those who witnessed this would see from what great evil the man had been delivered, and would believe in Christ because of the miracle" (*Explanation of the Holy Gospel According to St. Mark*, ch. 1).

St. Mark reports the people's astonishment: "And they were all amazed, insomuch that they questioned among themselves, saying, What thing is this? What new doctrine is this? for with authority commandeth He even the unclean spirits, and they do obey Him."

2

PETER'S MOTHER-IN-LAW (Mark 1)

The second miracle of St. Mark 1 is the healing of St. Peter's mother-in-law (vv. 29-31). It is recorded also in St. Matthew 8:14-15 and St. Luke 4:38-39. The three accounts are practically identical, but they vary in placement.

"And forthwith when they were come out of the synagogue, they entered into the house of Simon and Andrew, with James and John. But Simon's wife's mother lay sick of a fever, and anon they tell Him of her. And he came and took her by the hand, and lifted her up; and immediately the fever left her, and she ministered unto them" (Mark 1:29-31).

Brief though the story is, some of the Fathers find within it two important lessons, one concerning the spiritual life and the other a theological point.

St. Cyril of Alexandria, dealing with St. Luke's narration, interprets both lessons. Regarding the first, he says: "Let us, therefore, also receive Jesus; for when He has entered into us, and we have received Him into mind and heart, then He will quench the fever of unbefitting pleasures, and raise us up, and make us strong, even in things spiritual, so as for us to minister unto Him, by performing those things that please Him" (*Commentary on the Gospel of St. Luke*, ch. 4, vv. 38-39). The Fathers also observe that we, too, when the Lord has healed us in any way, are obliged to "minister," principally by means of service to our neighbors. (See especially the Blessed Theophylact, *Explanation of the Holy Gospel According to St. Mark*, ch. 1, vv. 29-31).

While St. Ambrose (*Treatise on the Gospel According to St. Luke*, Book 4, no. 63) sees in the mother-in-law's fever a symbol especially of our spiritual sickness (although she is not portrayed as a notorious sinner), St. Cyril notes that the Lord touched her hand and emphasizes the theological meaning behind that gesture:

"But observe again, I pray, how great is the efficacy of the touch of His holy flesh. For It both drives away diseases of various kinds, and a crowd of demons, and overthrows the power of the devil, and heals a very great multitude of people in one moment in time. And though able to perform these miracles by a word and the inclination of His will, yet to teach us something useful for us, He also lays His hands upon the sick. For it was necessary, most necessary, for us to learn that the holy flesh which He had made His own was endowed with the activity of the power of the Word by His having implanted in It a godlike might. Let It then take hold of us, or rather let us take hold of It by the mystical 'Giving of thanks' (the Eucharist), that It may free us also from the sicknesses of the soul, and from the assault and violence of demons" (op. cit.).

It is evident that in all these healings the Lord is moved with compassion, even if He is not yet ready to reveal Himself for who He is. St. Mark makes a statement of great importance: "He suffered not the demons to speak because they knew Him" (1:34). In the Synagogue, facing the man with an unclean spirit, Jesus had heard the spirit cry out, "I know who thou art, the Holy One of God." Jesus answered, "Hold thy peace." He was saying, in other words: "Be silent; I do not want you to confess me."

"He would not permit the unclean demons to confess Him; for it was not fitting for them to usurp the glory of the Apostolic office, nor with impure tongue to talk of the mystery of Christ. Yea! though they speak nothing that is true, let no one put credence in them; for the light is not known by the aid of darkness, as the disciple of Christ teaches us, where he says, 'For what communion hath light with darkness? or what consent hath Christ with Beliar?' (2 Corinthians 6:15)" (St. Cyril, op. cit.).

3

THE CLEANSING OF A LEPER (Mark 1)

The last miracle in St. Mark 1, the cleansing of a leper, appears also in the Gospels of St. Matthew (8:2-4) and St. Luke (5:12-15). All three Evangelists tell the story in more or less the same words, but here, as elsewhere, we find variation in the placement. St. Matthew puts the miracle after the Sermon on the Mount; he says, in fact, that it took place as soon as Jesus went down from the mountain (8:1). In neither St. Mark nor St.

Luke does the miracle appear to have any obvious connection with what precedes it.

All three writers quote the leper as saying, "If thou wilt, thou canst make me clean." This man has faith that Jesus is able to heal him if it is His will to do so. He sounds quite unlike the man who interceded for his son: "If thou canst do anything, have compassion on us, and help us" (Mark 9:22). St. Cyril of Alexandria comments: "The faith, however, of him who drew near is worthy of all praise, for he testifies that the Emmanuel can successfully accomplish all things, and seeks deliverance by His godlike commands, although his malady was incurable; for leprosy will not yield to the skill of physicians...Christ confirms his faith, and produces full assurance upon this very point. For He accepts His petition, and confesses that He is able, and says, 'I will; be thou cleansed'" (*Commentary on the Gospel of St. Luke*, ch. 5, v. 12). St. Athanasius, refuting the error of the Arians, writes: "We do not worship a creature...But we worship the Lord of creation, Incarnate, the Word of God. For if the flesh also is in itself a part of the created world, yet it has become God's body...The leper worshipped God in the Body, and recognized that He was God, saying, 'Lord, if thou wilt...' Neither by reason of the Flesh did he think the Word of God was a creature: nor because the Word was the maker of all creation did he despise the Flesh which He had put on. But he worshipped the Creator of the universe as dwelling in a created temple, and was cleansed" ("Letter LX," no. 3).

In all three Gospel accounts, we find that the Lord "put forth His hand, and touched him." Christ could have cured the man by a word or simply by His will, but He chooses to touch the leper. The action undoubtedly had a precise purpose. The Blessed Theophylact explains: "The Law forbade one to touch a leper, as he was unclean. But the Saviour touches the leper, showing that nothing is unclean by nature and that man ought to be set free from the observances of the Law, and that these observances applied only to man and not to God. Remember that Elisha had such reverence for the Law that he could not endure to see, let alone touch, Naaman who was a leper asking for healing (2/4 Kings 5:12)" (*The Explanation of the Holy Gospel According to St. Mark*, on ch. 1, vv. 41-42).

In each account of this miracle, we find that, after the man was cleansed, the Lord "straitly charged him, and forthwith sent him away; and saith unto him, See thou say nothing to any man; but go thy way, shew thyself to the priest, and offer for thy cleansing those things which Moses commanded, for a testimony unto them" (Mark 1:43-44; see Leviticus 14).

Whether the man misunderstood the Lord's command to say nothing to any man, or whether he blatantly disobeyed Him, we cannot know. It may be that he thought he was not to boast or draw attention to himself as someone particularly favored by the Lord. In any case, "He went out, and began to publish it much, and to blaze abroad the matter, insomuch that Jesus could no more openly enter into the city, but was without in desert places; and they came to Him from every quarter" (v. 45).

Apparently, the man did obey the second part of the command, for otherwise he would not have had the testimony that only the priest could give according to the Law. For St. Ambrose, it is highly significant that, in St. Matthew's Gospel, this encounter with the leper immediately follows the Sermon on the Mount. There the Lord declared that He had not come to destroy the Law and the prophets but to fulfill them" (5:17). St. Ambrose says: "This man who was cast out by the Law and now found himself cleansed by the Lord's power, must have understood that grace does not come from the Law, but that it is above the Law" (*Treatise on the Gospel According to St. Luke*, Book 5, no. 1).

So that it may not appear that the Lord despises the Law or is insensitive to the traditions it prescribes, and in order that the man may have the only credible testimony that he is indeed cleansed, Jesus conforms to the Law. "The Lord sends him to the priest. For the Law decreed that unless the priest declared the former leper to be clean, he was not permitted to enter the city, but was to be driven away. Jesus also commands him to offer the gift which those who had been cleansed were supposed to offer, so that the gift might be testimony that Jesus was not opposed to the Law. On the contrary, He held it in such high regard that He Himself commanded the very things that were prescribed by the Law" (The Blessed Theophylact, ibid., on vv. 43-45). The expression "for a testimony unto them" is explained by St. John Chrysostom in these terms: "For reproof, for demonstration, for accusation, if they (the priests, scribes and Pharisees) be unthankful. For since they said, as a deceiver and impostor we persecute Him as an adversary of God, and a transgressor of the Law" (*On the Gospel According to St. Matthew*, Homily 25, no. 3).

Recalling the leper's gratitude, evident in his publishing abroad the Lord's power, St. John Chrysostom urges us to remember always to be thankful for the benefits great and small that we and others receive from Him. "Therefore bearing these things in mind, let us also fulfill our duties to our neighbor, and to God let us give thanks continually. For it is too monstrous, enjoying as we do His bounty in deed every day, not so much as in word to acknowledge the favor; and this, though the acknowledgment again yield all its profit to us. Since He needs not, to be sure, anything of ours: but we stand in need of all things from Him. Thus thanksgiving itself adds nothing to Him, but causes us to be nearer to Him. For if men's bounties, when we call them to memory, do the more warm us with their love-charm, much more when we are continually bringing to mind the noble acts of our Lord towards us, shall we be more diligent in regard of His commandments" (ibid.).

4

THE MAN WITH A WITHERED HAND (Mark 3)

In the second chapter of St. Mark's Gospel, we find an account of the Lord's healing a man sick with the palsy. We have discussed this miracle in dealing with St. Matthew's account (9:1-8), which is the reading for the Sixth Sunday after Pentecost (see Part 1, ch. 4). This section of St. Mark (2:1-12) is read in our churches on the Second Sunday of the Great Fast.

Moving on, then, to St. Mark 3, we find the Lord healing a man with a withered hand. The miracle is found also in the two other synoptic Gospels (Matthew 12:9-13 and Luke 6:6-10), but neither version is among the Sunday lectionaries. The accounts of St. Mark and St. Luke are part of the Gospel readings for two Saturdays: St. Mark is read on the first Saturday of the Great Fast, St. Luke on the Saturday of the Twenty-first week after Pentecost. Saturday is appropriate for these lessons, as the healing they report took place on the Sabbath (seventh) day.

A number of the Fathers have left us interpretations of the miracle: among them are the Blessed Theophylact (dealing with St. Mark's account), St. Ambrose of Milan and St. Cyril of Alexandria (both treating St. Luke). All of them see a symbolic meaning in the healing of the withered hand. The hand, especially the right hand, bears much figurative significance in the Old Testament, where we find another notable case of a "withered" hand—that of King Jeroboam (1/3 Kings 13:4, 6).

The Blessed Theophylact says: "There was a time when our hands, that is, our strength to act, were sound, when there was not yet any transgression. But when the hand of man was stretched out to take the forbidden fruit, from that time on it withered and could not do good. But it will again be restored to its former health when we stand in the midst of the virtues" (*Explanation of the Holy Gospel According to St. Mark*, ch. 3, 1-5).

St. Cyril emphasizes that the Jews erroneously interpret the Sabbath law. "The Pharisees watched Him, to see if He would heal on the Sabbath; for such is the nature of an envious man, that he makes the praises given to others food for his own disease, and is wickedly maddened by their reputation. And what more did He say to this man, He who knows all things, Who searches the hearts and understands what is therein? 'For with Him is the Light,' as the Scriptures declare (Daniel 2:2). 'He spake to him that had the withered hand, Stand forth into the midst.' And why did He do this? It might be perhaps to move the cruel and unpitying Pharisee to compassion; the man's malady perhaps might shame them, and persuade them to allay the flame of envy" (*Commentary on the Gospel of St. Luke*, Homily 23).

St. Ambrose, commenting on the same passage in St. Luke, presents an interpretation that has much to say to us today:

"Then the Lord goes on to other works. For, having resolved to save the whole man, He covered all his members one by one, in such a way that He could say altogether truthfully: 'Are ye angry at me, because I made a man every whit whole on the Sabbath day?' (John 7:23). In this passage, then, the hand that Adam had stretched out to pick the fruit of the forbidden tree, He fills with the healthy and saving sap of good works, so that withered because of sin, it might be cured for good works. On this occasion, Christ demonstrates to the Jews that, by their false interpretations, they were violating the precepts of the Law, in judging that it was forbidden to perform even good works on the Sabbath. Since the Law, prefiguring in the present the features of the future, forbade bad works, not good ones. Then, if one is to rest from the works of this world, it is not an act empty of good works to rest in the praise of the Lord.

"You have heard the Lord's words, which say: 'Stretch forth thine hand.' Here we have the cure that is common to all. And you, who think you have a healthy hand, keep yourself free of avarice and sacrilege. Extend it frequently; extend it toward that poor man that implores you; extend it to help your neighbor, to take comfort to the widow, to snatch from injustice the very one whom you have subjected to a wicked anxiety; extend it toward God for your sins; thus, it is cured. Just as Jeroboam had his hand dried up (and was unable to withdraw it), when he was sacrificing to idols, and he was able to extend it and bring it back to himself when he prayed to God" (1/3 Kings 13:4, 6) (*Treatise on the Gospel of St. Luke*, Book 5, nos. 39-40).

5

THE CALMING OF THE TEMPEST (Mark 4)

Having healed the man with the withered hand, the Lord "healed many...who had plagues. And the unclean spirits, when they saw Him, fell down before Him, and cried, saying, 'thou art the Son of God'" (3:10-11). Just as when He healed the man with an unclean spirit (1:23-25) and Peter's mother-in-law (1:34), Jesus rejects the testimony that the devils and unclean spirits bear to His identity.

The next miracle in St. Mark's Gospel is the calming of the tempest (4:35-41). Both St. Matthew and St. Luke have accounts of the same event. All three are found in the weekday lectionary: St. Mark's on Wednesday of the fourteenth week after Pentecost, St. Matthew's (8:23-27) on Thursday of the second week, and St. Luke's (8:22-35) on Wednesday of the twenty-first week. The general plan for presenting the signs, wonders and miracles as an essential part of the proclamation of Christ remains at work on the weekdays after Pentecost, a period that we have called "the time of the Church's work in the world."

The three stories agree essentially, and the little ways in which they differ do not in any way diminish the importance of the event. To summarize: we find the Lord and His disciples in a boat crossing to the other side of the lake, and He has fallen asleep. A threatening storm arises. The disciples, in their alarm, awaken Him. He rebukes the wind, and the storm ceases. Jesus reprimands the disciples for having little or no faith. Little faith, but much amazement: "What manner of man is this, that even the wind and the sea obey Him?" they say (Matthew and Mark). "He commandeth the winds and water, and they obey Him" (Luke).

The holy Fathers of the Church write extensively about this miracle. St. Ambrose of Milan says: "You have read that He always spent the night in prayer. How is it that He remained sleeping during the storm? But this reveals the certainty of His power; for all were afraid, only He was calm...Although His body sleeps, His divinity acts; faith is active; therefore He says: 'Why are ye fearful, O ye of little faith?' (Matthew 8:26—similar to His reproach to Peter, Matthew 14:31). They deserved the reproach for having been afraid in the presence of Christ, since whoever clings to Him cannot perish...May He deign to still in us our violent storms, so that calm may return to our agitated lives, banishing our fear of shipwreck" (*Treatise on the Gospel According to St. Luke*, Book 6, nos. 42-43).

St. John Chrysostom sees a purpose behind the miracle. The Lord, he believes, is preparing His disciples for the dangerous trials they will face; He is assuring them of his power to protect them. Thereby their faith is built. "For great indeed were the former miracles too, but this one contained also in it a kind of discipline, and that no inconsiderable one, and was a sign akin to that of old (the crossing of the Red Sea). For this cause, He takes the disciples only with Himself, for as, when there was a display of miracles, He allows the people also to be present; so when trials and terrors were rising up against Him, then He takes with Him none but the champions of the whole world, whom He was to discipline" (*On the Gospel According to St. Matthew*, Homily 28, no. 1).

The Blessed Theophylact stresses the miracle's dogmatic implications: "When He awoke He rebuked first the wind (for it is the wind which causes the sea to become rough) and then the sea. He also rebukes the disciples for not having faith. For if they had faith, they would have believed that even while He was asleep He could keep them unharmed. They said to one another, 'What manner of man is this?' They still had doubts concerning Him. For when He calmed the sea by His command alone, and not with a rod, as did Moses, and not by an invocation of God, as did Elisha at the Jordan, and not with the ark, as did Joshua, the son of Nun, then they thought that He was more than a man; but when He slept, He appeared to them only as a man" (*Explanation of the Holy Gospel According to St. Mark,* ch. 4:35-41).

A footnote in the Chrysostom Press edition of Theophylact's commentary is worth considering: According to a "scholium" (a marginal annotation) in the Greek text, the Evangelist had good reason to add this detail. "He wished to show that, by divine ordering of events [lit. by economy], only the one boat was in danger of sinking."

If this be the case, there is another lesson for Christians today who find themselves in unfavorable circumstances. We often think that people around us, even unbelievers, enjoy a far more peaceful and unperturbed life. But Christians must have faith that adverse circumstances can be trials from the Lord that strengthen our faith and increase our dependence on Him and His power. We must not complain that following Christ brings no earthly rewards or perceptible benefit. Rather, in everything that happens to us, if we have committed ourselves to Him and belong to Him, we must, as St. Paul says, "understand what the will of the Lord is" (Ephesians 5:17).

6

THE DEMONIAC
THE RULER'S DAUGHTER
THE WOMAN WITH AN ISSUE OF BLOOD
(Mark 5)

Continuing our survey of the miracles in St. Mark, we come to the fifth chapter and find Jesus healing a man possessed. Jesus commands the demons to come out of him, and they plead to be sent into a herd of swine. The incident is often referred to as the miracle "of the Gadarene swine" (vv. 1-20).

All three synoptic Gospels include an account of this miracle (see Matthew 8:28-34 and Luke 8:26-39), and all are in the lectionary. St. Matthew's is read on the Fifth Sunday after Pentecost, St. Luke's on the twenty-third, and St. Mark's on the Thursday of the fourteenth week. Differences of detail were noted in Part 1, Chapter 3.

At this point we may take into account what two of the holy Fathers say about the man who was healed. First recall the words of St. Mark: "And when Jesus was come into the ship, he that had been possessed with the devil, prayed Him that he might be with Him. Howbeit Jesus suffered him not, but saith unto him, Go home to thy friends, and tell them how great things the Lord hath done for thee, and hath had compassion on thee. And he departed, and began to publish in Decapolis how great things Jesus had done for him, and all did marvel" (5:18-20).

The Blessed Theophylact explains the man's desire to be with Jesus: "He was afraid that the demons would find him alone and would again set upon him. But the Lord sends away to his own home, first of all, to show the man that even though He Himself is not present, His power and protecting care will keep him safe; and secondly, so that the man would bring benefit to those who would see him. And behold, the man began to proclaim and all men did marvel. See also the absence of boasting on the Lord's part. He did not say, 'Tell what great things I have done for thee,' but, 'Tell what great things the Lord hath done for thee.' So too, must you, O reader, attribute to God, and not to yourself, whatever good thing you have done" (*Explanation of the Holy Gospel According to St. Mark*, 5:14-20).

St. Ambrose, commenting on St. Luke's account, asks: "Why isn't the liberated man received (into His company), but is advised to return to his own home? Is it not to avoid an occasion for vainglory, but to show to the faithful that this dwelling is the natural law? Therefore, having obtained the remedy of his healing, it is prescribed that he return from the tombs and graves to this spiritual dwelling, so that what had been the sepulcher of his soul might become a temple of God" (*Treatise on the Gospel According to St. Luke*, Book 6, no. 53).

Further, the Lord's prescription may be seen as a kind of beginning of a lay apostolate. The man is told to bear witness to his transformation by the power of the Incarnate Word, first to those closest to him, his friends. Not every person who has come to know Christ is expected to become an ordained spokesman, but all Christians are expected to proclaim by a new life the One who has restored their "right mind" and true humanity, which is the human life in Christ.

In the same chapter (vv. 25-43), we read of the raising of the daughter of a ruler of the synagogue, along with the healing of a woman with an issue of blood. The same miracles are narrated in the other two synoptic Gospels (Matthew 9:18-26 and Luke 8:41-56). St. Luke's account is the Gospel reading appointed for the Twenty-fourth Sunday after Pentecost (see Part 1, ch. 12).

The woman had suffered twelve years and was healed, touching Jesus' garment, as He made His way to the house of Jairus, the ruler of the Synagogue. St. Ambrose, like other Fathers, sees her as a figure of the Church: "Why was Christ touched from behind? Could it be because it is written: 'Ye shall walk after the Lord your God' (Deuteronomy 13:4)? What is the meaning of the ruler's daughter's dying at the age of twelve and the woman's having suffered an issue of blood for twelve years? Is it not to make us understand that, while the Synagogue was in full vigor, the Church was suffering? (Note: the Church, by St. Ambrose's time, was almost totally Gentile; the Gentiles, before their evangelization, were the potential Church.) The defect of the one is the strength of the other, for 'through their fall salvation is come unto the Gentiles' (Romans 11:11), and the end of one is the beginning of the other—beginning not in nature's order, but with regard to salvation, for 'blindness in part is happened to Israel, until the fullness of the Gentiles be come in' (Romans 11:25). The Synagogue, then, is older than the Church, not in point of time, but insofar as salvation is concerned. While the first believed, the second did not believe and languished, captive of diverse illnesses of soul and body, without a healing remedy. They heard that the Jewish people were sick and they remained awaiting the remedy that would save it. They recognized that the time had come for the Physician from heaven to come. They arose to meet the Word. They saw that He was 'pressed' by a multitude. Those who 'press' do not believe, rather do those who touch. It is faith that touched Christ, faith that sees Him; their eyes do not perceive Him. For the one who looks without perceiving sees nothing; nor does the one (really) hear who does not understand what he hears, nor does he touch who does not touch with faith" (op. cit., no. 57).

7

FEEDING OF THE FIVE THOUSAND
JESUS WALKS ON THE SEA
THE DEAF AND DUMB MAN
(Mark 6-7)

The miracle narrated in St. Mark 6:34-44—the feeding of five thousand people—is recorded in the other three Gospels as well (Matthew 14:14-22; Luke 9:11-17; and John 6:1-14). St. Matthew's version is appointed to be read on the Eighth Sunday after Pentecost, St. John's (vv. 5-14) on the Wednesday of the Fifth Week of Pascha. We have dealt with St. Matthew's account (ch. 6) and with St. John's in our treatment of the signs (ch. 19).

St. Mark, like St. Luke, gives the initiative to the disciples; only St. Matthew apparently attributes it to the Lord Himself. The Fathers generally conclude that this is not a real difference. St. Mark and St. Luke simply begin with a concern already expressed by the Lord but restated by the disciples. His, certainly, was the compassion, the healing, and the teaching about the kingdom of God.

The miracle that follows is the Lord's walking on the sea (Matthew 14:22-34; Mark 6: 47-51; and John 6:16-21), on which we have already commented in Chapter 7. Only St. Mark's Gospel gives any indication that it was not until Jesus came to the disciples on the water and calmed the storm that they were able to overcome all their doubts about Him. "And they were so amazed in themselves beyond measure, and wondered. For they considered not the miracle of the loaves: for their heart was hardened" (6:51-52).

The Blessed Theophylact explains the last two verses of this story in this way: "To walk on water is a great miracle, and truly of God, and the storm and the contrary wind only add to the miracle. The apostles had not understood the miracle of the loaves, but through the miracle of the sea they understood. Hence it appears that Christ permitted them to be tested for this reason too, that since they had not recognized Who He was by the miracle of the loaves, they might do so by the miracle of the sea, and thus receive benefit" (*Explanation of the Holy Gospel According to St. Mark*, ch. 6).

In the last four verses of Chapter 6 (53-56), we learn that the people who followed the Lord brought the sick on beds and laid them in the streets and "besought Him that they might touch if it were but the border of His garment: and as many as touched Him were made whole."

The miracle related in St. Mark 7, in which Jesus heals the daughter of a woman, "a Greek, a Syrophoenician," is found also in St. Matthew 15:21-28 with the addition of many details (see the discussion in ch. 9):

"And again, departing from the coasts of Tyre and Sidon, He came unto the sea of Galilee, through the midst of the coasts of Decapolis. And they bring unto Him one that was deaf, and had an impediment in his speech; and they beseech Him to put His hand upon him. And He took him aside from the multitude, and put His fingers into his ears, and He spit, and touched his tongue; And looking up to heaven, he sighed, and saith unto him, Ephatha, that is, Be opened. And straightway his ears were opened, and the string of his tongue was loosed, and he spake plain" (7:31-35).

St. Matthew (9:32) and St. Luke (11:14) report a miracle that appears to be the same as this one, but neither refers to the man as deaf, only as mute. Neither mentions that the Lord put His fingers into the man's ears or that He touched the man's tongue with spittle. Both appear to be more concerned to report the accusation of the Pharisees (Matthew) or of "some of them" (Luke) that Jesus was "casting out devils through Beelzebub, the chief (prince) of the devils."

St. Mark's version, if indeed it speaks of the same miracle, is unique for these very details and deserves comment. The fullest explanation we have been able to find is the commentary of one Victor (called "Pseudo-Chrysostom"), a fifth-century presbyter of Antioch. Some of the same explanations are to be found in the Blessed Theophylact's commentary. According to Victor of Antioch: Jesus "takes the deaf and dumb person brought to Him, 'apart from the multitude,' not to perform His divine wonders openly; teaching us to put away vainglory and pride: for there is nothing through which a man works wonders more than by giving himself to humility and observing modesty. 'He put his fingers into his ears' Who could heal by a word; to show that the Body united to His Divinity, and to Its Operation, was endowed with the Divine power. Because of the sin of Adam, human nature had suffered much, and had been wounded in its senses and in its members. But Christ coming into the world revealed to us, in Himself, the perfection of human nature; and for this reason, He opened the ears with His fingers, and gave speech by the moisture of His tongue...He also groaned as taking our cause upon Himself; and as having compassion on human nature: seeing the misery into which humanity had fallen" (quoted in M. F. Toal, *The Sunday Sermons of the Great Fathers*, Volume 4, p. 2).

8

THE FEEDING OF THE FOUR THOUSAND
THE BLIND MAN
(Mark 8)

Continuing an exploration of the miracle accounts in St. Mark's Gospel, we come to 8:1-10, where we find the miraculous feeding of four thousand people. This section is the reading for Friday of the Sixteenth Week after Pentecost. St. Matthew is the only other Evangelist to record this incident.

There have been commentators, mostly modern, who think that this miracle is simply another version of the earlier one, at which five thousand were fed. We might dispute the identification of the two stories on the basis of details, but we also have the words of the Lord Himself as proof that they do not refer to the same event. Both in this Gospel (8:19-20) and in St. Matthew's (16:9-10), when the disciples forget to take bread with them after the second miracle, He asks them: "When I brake five loaves among five thousand, how many baskets full of fragments took ye up? And they say unto Him, Twelve. And when the seven among four thousand, how many baskets full of fragments took ye up? And they said, Seven." One extraordinary thing about this exchange is that, while Jesus usually refers to His miracles, signs, and wonders in a general way, here He speaks specifically of two.

The most obvious differences in the narrations of these miracles are the number of people fed, the number of loaves they had to begin with, and the number of baskets full of left-over fragments. St. John Chrysostom attaches no particular significance to the first two details but offers a simple explanation of the third. "In that case (of the five thousand), He makes the baskets full of fragments equal in number to His disciples, in this (the four thousand), the other baskets equal to the number of loaves" (*On the Gospel According to St. Matthew*, Homily 53, no. 2). He further concludes that Jesus, by His divine power, was able to provide exactly the amount of bread and fish not only to satisfy the multitude but also to fill the baskets of leftovers. The Blessed Theophylact finds symbolism in all the numbers: the four thousand that had been with Jesus three days are "those who have been baptized in three immersions, the seven loaves, things (or fruits) of the Holy Spirit (Galatians 5:22), seven being as well the number of completion and perfection; the five (of the five thousand), those enslaved by the five senses; and the four, those who practice the four virtues: courage, prudence, righteousness, and self-control" (*Explanation of the Holy Gospel According to St. Mark*, ch. 8). St. Cyril of Alexandria draws a moral lesson from the abundance of left-over fragments: Even he who gives or offers little will receive much in return (see his *Commentary on the Gospel of St. Luke*, ch. 9).

The eucharistic significance of both miracles has been discussed above in Chapter 6; that is, the feeding of so many is a sign of the miraculous feeding of the faithful of the Body and Blood of Christ. This interpretation is well attested by the Blessed Theophylact (*Explanation of the Holy Gospel According to St. Matthew*), St. Ambrose of Milan (*Treatise on the Gospel According to St. Luke*, Book 6, no. 84), and St. John Chrysostom (*On the Gospel According to St. John*, Homily 46).

The second miracle of St. Mark 8 (vv. 20-26) is the restoration of sight to a blind man of Bethsaida, a incident unique to this Gospel. Certain details of the narration evoke the Lord's scathing condemnation of that city along with Chorazin and Capernaum: "Woe unto thee, Chorazin! woe unto thee, Bethsaida! for if the mighty works had been done in Tyre and Sidon, which have been done in you, they had a great while ago repented, sitting in sackcloth and ashes. But it shall be more tolerable for Tyre and Sidon at the judgment than for you. And thou, Capernaum, which art exalted to heaven, shalt be thrust down to hell" (Luke 10:13-15). The denunciation of these cities was brought about because, although they were the places where "most of His mighty works were done, they repented not" (Matthew 11:20).

In view of this fact, the Blessed Theophylact interprets the miracle in this way: "The Lord, therefore, comes to Bethsaida, and the people bring a blind man unto Him. But the faith of those who bring the blind man was not genuine, which is why the Lord leads him out of the village and then heals him. He spits upon the eyes of the blind man, and puts His hands on him, so that we might learn that both the word of God as well as the action which follows the word are able to work miracles. For the hand is a symbol of action, and the spit is a symbol of the word, coming as it does from the mouth. The blind man himself did not have perfect faith, which is why the Lord does not at once make him to see clearly, but only in part, as his faith was only in part. For healing occurs according to one's faith. The Lord commands the man not to go back into the village, because, as I have mentioned, the inhabitants of Bethsaida were unbelieving and would have caused harm to the soul of the man. The Lord also commands him not to tell anyone what was done to him, lest, by not believing him, the villagers draw down upon themselves greater condemnation. And how often are we not also spiritually blind, living in the village, that is, in this world? But when Christ leads us out of the village, that is, from the world and its affairs, then we are healed. But after we have been healed, He tells us to return no more into the village, but to our home. For the home of each one of us is heaven and the dwelling places there" (*Explanation of the Holy Gospel According to St. Mark*, ch. 8, vv. 22-26).

EPILOGUE

The two remaining miracles of Christ recorded in St. Mark's Gospel are found in St. Matthew and St. Luke as well, and we have discussed them previously. One is the healing of a man's son, "which had a dumb spirit" (Mark 9: 17-31); the other is the restoration of sight to "blind Bartimaeus" (10:47-52).

The first miracle (as recounted by St. Matthew) is read on the Tenth Sunday after Pentecost (see ch. 8) and again (as recounted by St. Luke) on the Saturday of the Twenty-fifth Week after Pentecost. The second miracle account, from St. Mark, is the Gospel reading for the fourth Sunday of the Great Fast. St. Matthew's rendition of the same is read on the Saturday of the Twelfth Week after Pentecost; St. Luke's is read on the Thirty-first Sunday (see ch. 15).

Without touching upon the great miraculous events of our Savior's life among men—His birth, transfiguration, resurrection, and ascension—most of which are occasions for the Great Feasts of the Church, we have treated most of the miracles, wonders, and signs performed by the Lord and recorded in the four Gospels.

Since many of the Lord's cures and healings are referred to in broadly inclusive statements, such as "He healed many that were sick of diverse diseases, and cast out many devils" (Mark 1:34; Matthew 4:23; Luke 5:15), it is obvious that it would be impossible to treat all of the wonders that the Lord performed. Even St. John acknowledges that Jesus did many things not included in his Gospel (20:30 and 21:25).

We shall try now, with the Lord's help, to make a few summarizing observations concerning all of the foregoing discussions, which we have divided into three sections in the interest of locating them in relation to the liturgical experience of the people of God. With this in mind, we will note that, *in general*, the lessons from St. Matthew and St. Luke are read on the thirty-two Sundays after Pentecost, those from St. Mark during the Great Fast, and those from St. John during the Paschal season.

The miracles, wonders, and signs wrought by our Lord Jesus Christ were not always simple demonstrations of His mighty power. Only a few of them were, in fact. And those few did verify His divine lordship over all.

Jesus healed sicknesses and cast out demons. He gave sight to the blind and fed thousands. He raised the dead. He taught the living. Behind every action lay His great love and compassion. "When He saw the multitude, He was moved with compassion on them, because they fainted, and were scattered abroad, as sheep having no shepherd" (Matthew 9:36; see also 14:14 and 20:34; Mark 1:41, 5:19, and 6:34; and Luke 7:13). We include teaching among the things that the Lord did for the people, because what they needed, even more than physical healing, was the knowledge of God. For what will it profit a man if he gains his health and loses his soul? If Jesus made us physically whole but did not bring us to a relation with God, our lives would remain meaningless. Recall that on one occasion, when urged to heal a man sick of the palsy, the Lord first forgave the man's sins. Only then, to demonstrate that He had power to forgive sins, did He tell the man to take up his bed and walk.

St. John Chrysostom calls our attention to another significant reason for the miracles: "You see how again He in due season reminds them of His passion, laying up for them great store of comfort from the passion of John (the Baptist). And not just by saying that " 'the Son of Man should likewise suffer (at the hands of the scribes and Pharisees),' but also by presently (at the same time) working great miracles. Yes, and whenever He speaks of His passion, at the same time He works miracles, both after those sayings and before them...for instance, on the mountain, when He had shown them the marvelous vision, and the prophets had been discoursing of His glory, He reminded them of His passion...and after a little while again, when He had cast out the devil, which His disciples were not able to cast out; for then too, 'As they abode in Galilee,' so it says, 'Jesus said unto them, The Son of Man shall be betrayed unto the hands of sinful men, and they shall kill Him, and the third day He shall rise again' " (*On the Gospel According to St. Matthew*, Homily 57, no. 2). The disciples needed to know, when the Lord was foretelling his suffering and death, that He had all power, that His passion was voluntary, that He would undergo it all for the life of the world.

The second section of our study consisted of an explanation of the wondrous works of our Lord Jesus Christ that are found in the Holy Gospel According to St. John. The Evangelist consistently calls them "signs" (Greek, *semeia*) rather than "miracles" (*dynameis*), the term used generally in the other Gospels (John 2:11; 3:2; 4:54; 6:14; 7:31; 20:30, etc.). While all of the "miracles, wonders, and signs" attest to the Lord Jesus Christ, His oneness with the Father, His mighty power, and His mission (see Acts 2:22-40), St. John's treatment is unique. He shows that they have a significance beyond that of demonstrating the Lord's power.

With few exceptions, the Gospel lessons for the Paschal season are taken from St. John. Following the pattern established in Part 1, we treated the signs within the framework of the Church's liturgical experience. From the early days of the Church's mission to the world, Pascha, being the celebration of Christ's victory over death, was the most appropriate time for the baptism of new members. In this holy mystery, His death, burial, and resurrection became their own; His victory became theirs (see Romans 6:3-5; Colossians 2:12). Once the catechumens were baptized after a long period of instruction, they were further taught in the doctrine of Christ, the transforming power of His presence as He performed the signs, and the continuation of that very presence in the holy mysteries. St. Cyril of Jerusalem, in his *Catechetical Lectures*, calls attention to the fact that his postbaptismal instruction is designed to explore the deep meaning of those mysteries that the newly baptized received at Pascha. Having received God's grace in baptism, chrismation, and the eucharist, they are capable of understanding what they could not have fully understood before.

The details and circumstances that attend the discourses in St. John's Gospel show that Jesus' "signs" testify to His truth, identity, and purpose. Most of these details and explanations are not included in the synoptic accounts of the same miracles. And St. John includes miracles that the others do not: the changing of water to wine at the wedding feast at Cana and the raising of Lazarus. St. John had something of an advantage over the other Evangelists, perhaps. He wrote later, after a longer experience of life and worship within the Church. He could see more clearly the theological implications of the events of our Lord's life. He knew what the sign at Cana meant, theologically. He perceived the eucharistic significance of the discourse that followed the feeding of the five thousand. The "water" signs pointed to the "laver of regeneration." The raising of Lazarus anticipated the Lord's own rising and the general resurrection.

To complete our study, we provided a third section to survey the miracles and signs not included in the first two. Although some of these, principally from St. Mark's Gospel, are part of the lectionary, they do not seem to follow the clear and obvious pattern we find in the lessons for the Paschal season and the Sundays after Pentecost. Readings from St. Mark do predominate, however, during the Great Fast on days when the Divine Liturgy may be celebrated, as well as on the weekdays during the period of preparation. We may briefly summarize what is read from St. Mark at the Liturgy. Five of the nine readings are miracle accounts: a man with a withered hand healed on the Sabbath (2:23-3:5) on St. Theodore Saturday; a leper cleansed (1:35-44) on Saturday of the Second Week; a paralytic healed (2:1-12) on the Second Sunday; a deaf man healed (7:31-37) on Saturday of the Fourth Week; and a possessed man healed (9:17-31) on the Fourth Sunday. The others contain: the story of the call of four of the disciples (2:14-17), Saturday of the Third Week; the Lord's teachings about the essence of true commitment or discipleship (8:34-9:1), Third Lenten Sunday; the ill-conceived request of James and John (10:32-45), the Fifth Sunday; and the last two of these, the Lord's foretelling of His betrayal, trial, death, burial, and resurrection.

In view of one of the essential themes of the Great Fast, "the recovery by us of what we were made through our own baptismal death and resurrection," (Father Alexander Schmemann, *Great Lent*, p. 14), we undertake to relearn the basics of our faith and to absorb the truth of the proclamation of Christ—His person, His mission, and His all-sufficient sacrifice. Of these things, the lessons of St. Mark provide a brief but adequate summary.

We conclude with a final thought drawn from the final Gospel, St. John's. All of the miracles, wonders, and signs of Christ are evidence that He is indeed the Son of God, the Redeemer and Savior of the world, the anticipated Messiah, the One whom we, with St. Thomas, confess to be "my Lord and my God" (John 20:28). St. John emphasizes one detail and not another, he underlines things that the other Evangelists omit, he sometimes puts events in something other than chronological order. We think that he had his reasons, and that he hints at them even as he spells out what motivated him to write the Gospel that bears his name. "And many other signs truly did Jesus in the presence of His disciples, which are not written in this book: but these are written, that ye might believe that Jesus is the Christ, the Son of God; and that believing ye might have life through His name" (20:30-31).